DATE DUE

JUL 1 6 2019			
			PRINTED IN U.S.A.

ADVANCE PRAISE FOR SAVVY

Savvy could not be more timely. It is all our responsibility to learn how to navigate the digital information minefield and seek out the truth. Bravo Rohini and Shiv for giving us an essential guidebook to do it.

—SATJIV CHAHIL, Former Chief Marketing Officer, Apple Inc.

A must-read for any leader or company that strives toward meaning and authenticity.

—ANTONIO LUCIO, Global Chief Marketing Officer, Facebook

Savvy - a perfect title for this fascinating book - opens our eyes and minds to the hidden psychological effects that drive our decisions, sometimes to our regret. I enthusiastically recommend this wise and well-written book.

—OSCAR G. CHASE, Russell D. Niles Professor of Law, New York University School of Law

As the distinction between what's news, opinion, propaganda and lies becomes harder and harder to determine, there could not be a better time for Savvy. A must-read for anyone who puts trust over populism.

—BRAD JAKEMAN, Senior Advisor & Former President, Global Beverages, PepsiCo

Having confidence and trust in customers, employees and investors is the foundation of any company. Shiv and Rohini's book, Savvy, is very timely given the current environment in which we live and communicate.

—MICHAEL KNEELAND, CEO United Rentals Inc., a Fortune 500 company

A thoughtful treatment of the way in which the modern information ecosystem exacerbates our cognitive biases, making us ever more vulnerable to believing false information and eroding trust in key institutions.

—JENNIFER KAVANAGH PhD, Senior Political Scientist, Rand Corporation

Savvy asks us to pay attention to what we are being fed and how we are digesting it. It is a superb manifesto that arms us with perspectives and tools so we can truly thrive in today's "post-trust" but still very real world.

—**RISHAD TOBACCOWALA,** Chief Growth Officer, Publicis Groupe

It's depressing that this book had to be written, but we're very lucky that it was. Shiv Singh and Rohini Luthra deliver a fascinating, insightful and practical handbook for our times. However savvy you think you are, you'll be a lot savvier for reading this.

—**CINDY GALLOP,** Founder & CEO, MakeLoveNotPorn

Facts should not be open to interpretation. Shiv and Rohini share how we can identify our own biases and see opportunities in a new way ... to face the facts, to help us learn and grow, and to become part of a more collaborative, productive and progressive society. We're all just human after all. We thrive together. We fall together.

—**BRIAN SOLIS,** Digital anthropologist, futurist, & bestselling author of *Lifescaling: How to be Creative in an Era of Distraction*

If you care about the future of our post-truth world, Savvy is a must-read both professionally and personally. It illuminates how to combat the powerful psychological biases that lead us away from the truth.

—**SUSAN MACDERMID,** Founder, Ascendant Network

"Navigating Fake Companies, Fake Leaders and Fake News?" Yes, please! At a time when we have plenty of all three ruining our political and business landscape, Singh and Luthra have given us a guide to fighting back and making smarter decisions with this timeliest of books.

—**SREE SREENIVASAN,** Founder of Digimentors & former Professor at the Columbia School of Journalism

We face a crisis of trust because people feel there is no longer any truth. Singh and Luthra have written a highly-readable analysis of how it happened and how we might return truth to its necessary prominence in a social media-infused society. An urgently needed book.

—**DAVID KIRKPATRICK,** Author of *The Facebook Effect* & founder of Techonomy Media

SHIV B. SINGH &
ROHINI LUTHRA, PhD

SAVVY

NAVIGATING FAKE COMPANIES,

FAKE LEADERS

AND FAKE NEWS

IN THE POST-TRUST ERA

IDEAPRESS
PUBLISHING

Proudly printed in the United States by Ideapress Publishing.

IDEAPRESS PUBLISHING | WWW.IDEAPRESSPUBLISHING.COM

All trademarks are the property of their respective companies.

COVER DESIGN BY JEFF MILLER

First Printing: January, 2019

Cataloging-in-Publication Data is on file with the Library of Congress.

ISBN: 978-1-940858-72-2

SPECIAL SALES
Ideapress Books are available at a special discount for bulk purchases for sales promotions and premiums, educational institutions or for use in corporate training programs. Special editions, including personalized covers, custom forewords and bonus content are also available. For more information, email info@ideapresspublishing.com

For those who believe truth will prevail.

TABLE OF CONTENTS

• • • • •

PREFACE

● ● ● ● ●

Shiv: I've spent most of my career believing in the power of social media to change the world for the better. You could say I was a little naive.

Traveling the four corners of the world, I advised the largest global companies on how to adapt to the social media era, recommending how to build and market new products to reach customers living so much of their lives in the social media world. It was a thrilling time. I was such a believer that I even wrote the book *Social Media Marketing for Dummies,* which was updated twice and translated into several languages due to demand. Later, when I went to work for PepsiCo and then Visa, I urged those companies to embrace social media marketing.

Then the revelations of abuses began breaking fast and furiously. Few could have foreseen that Russians would use social media to interfere with the 2016 US presidential election. Nor could many have anticipated the genocide in Myanmar caused by bad actors with new communication tools. We are now more aware that electronic communication in its many forms has been strangling quality journalism, aiding the creation and viral spread of fake news, and sowing increasingly heated dissension and endemic distrust. You only have to Google the term, deepfakes, to see the worst of it.

Some say the rancor and rampant mendacity isn't all social media's fault. While it is easy to blame the platforms for the pickle we find ourselves in, the technology itself is neutral, and those who created it have, by and large, had noble ambitions. They have done an immense amount of good for the world as well.

It's not all the fault of us users who've been duped either. We are in uncharted territory. We're stumbling on the pitfalls as we discover the joys of the new tools, getting a difficult education in the many new ways information can be weaponized by bad actors. Our governments have arguably been slow to learn. With their training wheels still on, they are only beginning to determine the regulations they must enact. But recriminations are not solutions. What is vital now is that we appreciate the seriousness of the problem and learn to protect ourselves and combat the abuses.

The stark reality is that we have entered what we will describe in this book as a new *post-trust era*, in which telling truth from opinion, and separating fact from outright fabrications, requires us to be on guard, intensely aware of the ways in which we are being played and how we are unwittingly contributing to the problem. That's all the more difficult because we increasingly reside in echo chambers that reinforce our views and cater to our biases, widening the gap of opinion and making civil, fact-based discussion of issues extremely challenging. Fakery has not only pervaded politics, it has made deeper inroads into business and our personal lives. Our business leaders aren't as trustworthy as we once believed, with companies more regularly falling prey to scandal, and friends and relatives find themselves aligned in hostile opposing camps. This post-trust era is frightening.

I co-authored this book because I deeply believe that we can move beyond this era to a future in which we re-establish high standards and restore trust. We can become savvy about the range of abuses and about our vulnerabilities to manipulation so that we are able to avail ourselves of the wonderous benefits of social media and the new breed of technologies rapidly developing without falling prey. Despite their significant drawbacks, social media and the retinue of other new communication tools have changed the world mostly for the better. As they've changed the world, we humans are changing in some ways too. But it is imperative that as we change we don't lose sight of the fundamental binding agent of human society - our ability to build and sustain trusted relationships not only with people who look and sound like us but also the ones who don't; to build relationships founded upon integrity, sincerity and the truth. These are the relationships that stand the test of time, whether they were formed in the physical world or the digital one, in the workplace or in the home, during our childhood or in our adult life.

The onus is on us to make sure that the post-trust era isn't a lasting one. Each of us can do more ourselves to make sure that it isn't, and that is what this book is about. I hope *Savvy* will help you in your journey out of the post-trust era.

Rohini: As a psychologist, I've devoted my professional career to helping people uncover their truths. I've found that the truth of one's life is often elusive; taking time, introspection, and effort to discover. I've also seen that 'truth' is not an absolute, fixed construct. Your version of an event may look completely different from mine. What appears white to some, looks black to others, and all shades of gray to the rest. A psychologist's job is to create a safe haven in which one's intimate truths—whatever shades they may be—can be revealed, understood and respected.

The notion that a person's truth is unique is nothing new. What is new is that we now have multiple and competing truths in all spheres of our lives: in the news, inside companies, in government, and within our circles of family and friends. Also, while fakery has been a feature of human life through the ages, technology and social media have turbocharged its spread.

My concern about the new intensity of fakery stems not only from my professional life but also from my most important job, as a mother to my two young sons. I want them to grow up believing that the truth matters. I want them to understand the responsibility they carry in critically analyzing all they see and hear. Only if they learn to question information—and their perceptions of it—will they stand a chance of successfully navigating the pitfalls of the post-truth era.

To help them (and myself) prepare for this challenge, I began turning to science to help understand the machinations of fakery. Surely, I thought, there must be some insight to be gleaned from the social sciences to guide us through these times. And indeed there was. For decades scientists have been studying why people fall for fakeness. In *Savvy*, we highlight seminal studies that illuminate how cognitive biases deeply ingrained in all of our minds distort our perceptions and lead us to privilege some information sources over others, trustworthy or not, and throw our trust behind people, groups and organizations that are deceiving us. We introduce them according to the underlying, largely subconscious, motivations behind the biases and offer advice about how we can recognize when we're falling into their grip and overcome them.

I, like Shiv, am an optimist and believe we can successfully navigate this complex post-truth terrain. After all, while the unbridled fakery is undermining our trust in information and the sources of it, we continue to fundamentally trust one another in so many ways. We let strangers use our homes when we travel, we sit in unknown people's cars and allow them to drive us to our destinations, and we depend on anonymous reviews more than ever when making purchases. All is not lost in the post-trust era. We can forge our way to a new savvy era. I hope this book plays a small part in getting us there.

INTRODUCTION

● ● ● ● ●

FAKE NEWS IS OLD NEWS

Fake news is nothing new. Misinformation, false information, and propaganda have all been around as long as news itself. Over three hundred years ago, in 1672, King Charles II of England issued a proclamation to, "Restrain the spreading of false news and licentious talking of matters of state and government."[1] He was nervous about anti-government conversations brewing in the coffee houses of London. He ordered that all the coffee houses be shut down within twelve days. It was an unmitigated financial disaster for cafe owners and a major setback for free speech. It ultimately did nothing, though, to dampen enthusiasm for fake news.

Nor did other early efforts. The first newspaper published in North America was launched in Boston on September 25, 1690. Titled *Publick Occurrences Both Forreign and Domestick*, the newspaper would appear monthly, readers were told, unless "any glut of global occurrences happen oftener." The first edition was all of four 6 by 10-inch pages (with only three of the pages filled in). Just four days after its launch, the newspaper was shut down on orders of the colonial government. No other issues were printed. The Governor and Council found the newspaper to contain "sundry doubtful and uncertain reports" and therefore "manifest and declare their high resentment and disallowance of said pamphlet, and order that the same be suppressed and called in."[2] Of course, fake news in America (and much of the rest of the world as well) would go on to thrive.

Source: Massachusetts Historical Society

Every generation before us has been subject to rampant fake news. Blatant fakery tainted the coverage of what was probably the first event to become major news all over the world—the Great Lisbon

Earthquake. Shysters shamelessly used the tragedy as an opportunity to make false accusations of blame. The quake struck on the morning of November 1, 1755, All Saints' Day in the Kingdom of Portugal. Seismologists today estimate its magnitude was in the range of 8.5 to 9.0. Eighty-five percent of Lisbon's buildings were destroyed and somewhere between ten thousand and one hundred thousand people died, making it one of the deadliest earthquakes in history. The consequences were far-reaching, exacerbating political tensions and disrupting the Kingdom's colonial ambitions, eventually leading to the decline of Portugal as a colonial empire.[3]

The Catholic Church and other European authorities blamed the disaster on divine retribution against sinners, calling the quake a sign of God's rage against the atheists and freethinkers of Lisbon. An entire genre of fake news pamphlets (relações de sucessos) emerged, both in Portugal and across Europe, claiming that survivors owed their lives to an apparition of the Virgin Mary. The prominent philosopher Voltaire attacked the fallacious claims, making him an early anti-fake activist.[4]

Fake news has persisted largely because it is such good business. Major news empires have been built on it. Today's media fabricators have nothing over two of the most successful fake news purveyors in history, William Randolph Hearst, owner of the New York Journal, and Joseph Pulitzer, owner of the New York World. These two titans, known for their blatant disregard of responsible journalism, faced off at the turn of the 20th century. The two men were in a circulation war, each trying to out sensationalize, and outsell, the other. They saw conflict as a way to sell newspapers, and both men were willing to conjure up stories where real ones didn't exist. They published exaggerated, or even completely fabricated, accounts of alleged atrocities committed by the Spanish military against the citizens of Cuba. Hearst and Pulitzer, in their two-man circulation war, have been credited with leading the US into the Spanish-American War. [5]

A particularly ghoulish use of fake news was perpetrated in Indonesia in the aftermath of the 30 September Movement. A pro-communist group of Indonesian military personnel kidnapped and assassinated six generals in the early hours of October 1, 1965. They took President Sukarno under their protection and grabbed control of key media outlets. However, the head of the army's strategic military reserve command, General Suharto, responded decisively and defiantly. By the end of the day, the coup attempt was squashed, and General Suharto had taken control of the country.

The swirling of fabrications that followed was dizzying. Using the attempted coup as a pretext, General Suharto triggered a purge of communist sympathizers across Indonesia. By spreading fake news that the kidnapped generals had been sexually mutilated and tortured by young communist women before they were killed, he whipped the population into a frenzy. Over the next six months he used wildly inaccurate anti-communist information as a weapon to instigate his supporters to massacre more than five hundred thousand suspected communists.[6] The purveyors of fake news have much blood on their hands.

In each of these cases, as today, information was molded and disseminated by business or religious leaders, governments, or news outlets with highly specific agendas. Fake news weaponizes information and the public is dangerously vulnerable to its manipulations, often unable to determine whom and what to believe. The end result is that fake news makes it difficult to be savvy.

OUR INSTITUTIONS HAVE FAILED US

Empires have crumbled, important scientific discoveries have been ignored or denigrated, once powerful and respected businesses have gone bankrupt and famines have struck — all due to falsehoods. What's particularly troubling about fake news today is that never before has there been the technology to so quickly and persuasively disseminate it. The current flourishing of fakeness is more insidious and widespread than ever, perpetrated not only by political figures and other authorities, but broadly by members of the public, on social media, and by companies too. We need look no further than the saga of Theranos, the defunct blood-testing firm, to see how blatant fraud can be so easily carried out by business leaders, even as they become media heroes. We will explore this story in more depth in Chapter 3.

People have always gravitated toward information that resonates, shrugging off tidings that don't. We feel comfortable in the echo chambers of our information silos. And today, technology allows for much more precise thin-slicing and targeting of information. It also gives fabrications much greater reach and makes them more compelling. Falsifications travel faster than ever before, and as they build momentum they also gain credibility.

In March 2018, a landmark research study conducted at the Massachusetts Institute of Technology revealed that fake news actually travels faster than real news. The study analyzed every major news story in

English published on Twitter since the platform was launched. This was roughly 126,000 news stories, tweeted by three million users from 2006 through 2017. Not only did falsifications rip around faster, they reached more people by penetrating deeper into social networks.[7] The findings were presciently anticipated by British social critic Jonathan Swift, who, in 1710, wrote, "Falsehood flies, and the truth comes limping after."

The walls separating fact from manipulated fiction are crumbling, and it is difficult to know whom to trust and what to believe. Our companies, leaders, and media have failed us. Technology is certainly not solely to blame for today's fakery epidemic, but it has put it on steroids. The result is that we have entered a post-truth era.

On November 16, 2016, Oxford Dictionaries named "post-truth" its international word of the year, reflecting what it referred to as a "highly charged" political twelve months. In choosing the word, the editors defined post-truth as a state in which "objective facts are less influential in shaping public opinion than appeals to emotion and personal belief." While the first usage of the term dates to 1992, frequency of its use increased by two *thousand* percent between 2015 and 2016.[8] But post-truth isn't just a word that's suddenly gotten popular. It describes a new condition of the time we are living in - one with deeply troubling ramifications.

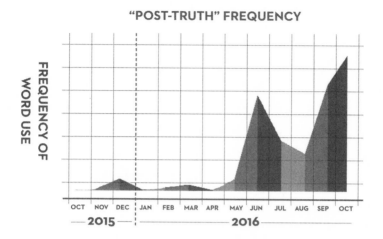

"POST-TRUTH" FREQUENCY

Source: Oxford Dictionary - https://en.oxforddictionaries.com/
word-of-the-year/word-of-the-year-2016

Navigating this post-truth era is getting harder by the day - we cannot begin to imagine what it will be like when our children are grown. Increasing automation, empowered by artificial intelligence, will make manipulations of us even more compelling. In turn, discerning what to trust will be even harder. This new era is quickly hurtling towards us. In this fast-approaching world, our cars will drive our children to school without us there, robots will be our bosses (and conduct performance reviews), governments will have more real-time data about us than we do ourselves, and our artificial intelligence personal assistants will choose what we get to read and what we never see. In this world, which is less than a decade away, we will need to be extremely savvy. As a husband-and-wife team, one of us a corporate executive and the other a clinical psychologist, we look at our children and wonder about the world they will inherit and how they will cope. We used to believe as parents we would have all the answers for them. But with the rapidly changing technology landscape, we simply don't.

But do not despair! Those of us who want to protect ourselves from fakery and to combat it are not altogether powerless. We can learn to understand the dynamics driving fakeness and employ an arsenal of tools to inoculate ourselves, and for business leaders, to protect our teams and companies. That is the aim of Savvy. Combining our professional expertise — in psychology for Rohini and in business and technology for Shiv — we draw upon the rich academic traditions of behavioral and social psychology, media studies and management. We introduce seminal scientific research and diagnose a wealth of cases of fakeness in order to illuminate why so many forms of fakeness are so compelling, and how to spot them.

We cover a wide range of fakery, addressing not only fake news, but deception in the halls of politics and business too. Each domain of fakeness merits multi-volume tomes of its own, and a few books have already been published that look at fake business leaders, fake politicians, and fake news in isolation. We have covered the topics together because the same underlying machinations are involved in perpetrating deception, and falling prey to it, across these domains. The more we researched, the more we saw the parallels among fakeness in companies, the political sphere, and in the news.

This book isn't meant to be comprehensive. We could not possibly cover *all* of the studies that inform human fakeness, nor, of course, highlight every instance of egregious deception by political, business, and media figures. We have not addressed in detail how governments and companies should devise systems to combat fakery. There are a number of ways in which societies have grappled with the problems of false information, mistruths, and propaganda. Many good solutions have been proposed. More transparency among companies, leaders, and media outlets is one notable example, which we salute. We need to have more fact-checking organizations, better data controls, and government regulations. But this book is not about how the world must change in order to stamp out fakery. Instead we will focus on how each of us must respond to this world in order to survive and maintain our sanity.

Savvy is about understanding the role we (as consumers of information) play in succumbing to *and* propagating fakeness. We will share a proven method for how to recognize disingenuous information and faulty thinking patterns so that you can orient yourself toward the truth. Just as we have technology glitches so too do we have human glitches in the way we process information. These glitches distort our judgments and make us fall prey to fakeness. These "glitches" are organized by chapter within which we've selected foundational studies and stories that are topical in order to offer a quick, and we hope engaging, tour d'horizon of the pitfalls and how to avoid them.

NAVIGATING THE BOOK

In the next chapter, we examine the psychology of trust and how the post-truthiness of today is leading to a crisis of trust, including both a lack of trust in credible sources and institutions and an excess of trust in unreliable ones. We cover landmark studies that illuminate how trust is fostered and the disturbing consequences when trust is eroded.

Within the chapters that follow, we introduce psychology studies and examples from today's headlines to explore why we human beings are so vulnerable to putting our trust in people, organizations and information that are biased, or outright deceptive, and on the flip side, to doubting credible sources. We often fall for fakery because, as psychologist Dan Ariely puts it, we are "predictably irrational".[9] We have a number of innate biases that make us vulnerable to accepting *and* spreading false information. Revealing the workings of a range of these cognitive glitches, we provide guidance on how to be alert when we may be falling prey to them. At the end of each chapter, practical tips are offered for how to override these biases.

In the final chapter, we focus on the future and consider how governments and technology companies are gaining new capabilities for gathering information about us - automating our world in ways that will present new and even greater challenges regarding who and what we should trust. Introducing a number of developments, such as China's "social credit system," we delve into how our lives may become increasingly controlled in ways that we haven't even begun to imagine.

We are at a critical time in history. We must become more alert about how vulnerable we are to fall prey to fakeness. At the same time, we need to be mindful of the role we play in sometimes unwittingly condoning or promoting fakery. We don't have to buy in to post-truth as a fait accompli; we can protect ourselves and help protect our companies, communities, and loved ones as well.

CHAPTER 1

WE DON'T TRUST ANYMORE

"We inhabit a climate of trust as we inhabit an atmosphere
and notice it as we notice air, only
when it becomes scarce or polluted."
—Annette Baier, philosopher

GLOBAL STRESSES

WE ARE LIVING IN A TIME OF GREAT CONTRADICTION. ON ONE HAND, we are living longer, healthier lives. Child mortality rates are the lowest they've ever been. We're richer and more robust than our ancestors. Medical advancements have eradicated diseases that used to ravage continents, killing thousands in one fell swoop. Technological advances have made our world small, allowing us to talk to anyone, anywhere while even translating our words into virtually any language in real time. We're on the verge of space tourism, self-driving vehicles, and artificial intelligence machines that teach themselves to solve our most complex problems. Any visitor from another planet should be suitably impressed with our progress.

Then again, maybe we haven't progressed all that much. Safety concerns, access to health care, government corruption, religious conflicts, and global warming undermine the strides we've made. And sadly that list goes on. In several parts of the world, freedom of the press is under attack. Steps have been taken to weaken and even dismantle independent judiciaries elsewhere. Basic human rights are taking a backseat to political and economic calculations for far too many leaders in far too many countries. We turn a blind eye just as easily as we did hundreds of years ago to famine, genocide, mass incarcerations, and race-driven violence. The only difference now is our technological advances in global communication don't allow us to feign ignorance when we do nothing about the problems. Earth is being destroyed, not by an unstoppable natural disaster, but at our own hands, by the choices we make, the fuels we burn, what we buy, how we dispose of our waste, and the cavalier ease with which we ignore the alarm bells of climate change. Yes, there's a lot wrong with the world today.

Any number of explanations can be given for this contradiction. But for us, one stands out. We're experiencing a massive breakdown of trust in the institutions that govern over societies. We are in a crisis of trust. On the one hand, we're not trusting information and people that we should. In September 2018, UN Secretary-General António Guterres declared the world "is suffering from a bad case of 'Trust Deficit Disorder.'[1] Yet, on the other hand, we're placing too much trust in sources we should be wary of.

THE STATE OF TRUST

Every year (for the last eighteen years), Edelman, a global communications firm, conducts a global trust and credibility survey. Thirty-three thousand respondents from twenty-eight countries are asked the same questions year to year about the level of trust they have in governments, non-governmental organizations, businesses and the media. The Edelman Trust Barometer results are released at the World Economic Forum in January and the survey is followed closely by the leaders of Fortune 500 companies, national governments, the United Nations and the International Monetary Fund. We've been following the study since its inception and found the 2017 results deeply troubling.

Trust in institutions has been steadily dropping, but the 2017 Trust Barometer showed dramatic declines across the board in every facet tracked by the study. They occurred in almost all of the countries surveyed, and the numbers did not rebound in 2018. In only four countries did those surveyed express more trust than distrust in their institutions—China, Indonesia, India and the United Arab Emirates. In four others, respondents expressed neutral relationships with their institutions, neither more trusting nor distrusting of them—Singapore, Mexico, the Netherlands and Malaysia. For the remaining twenty countries, the distrusters outweighed the trusters, and, for some countries and institutions, the declines were in the double digits.[2]

2017 General Population		2018 General Population	
47	Global	48	Global
72	India	74	China
69	Indonesia	71	Indonesia
67	China	68	India
60	Singapore	66	UAE
60	UAE	58	Singapore
53	The Netherlands	54	Mexico
52	Mexico	54	The Netherlands
52	U.S.	53	Malaysia
50	Colombia	49	Canada
49	Canada	47	Argentina
48	Brazil	47	Colombia
48	Italy	47	Spain
48	Malaysia	46	Turkey
45	Argentina	45	Hong Kong
44	Hong Kong	44	Brazil
44	Spain	44	S. Korea
43	Turkey	43	Italy
42	Australia	43	U.S.
42	S. Africa	41	Germany
41	Germany	41	Sweden
40	France	40	Australia
40	U.K.	40	France
38	S. Korea	39	Poland
37	Sweden	39	U.K.
36	Ireland	38	Ireland
35	Japan	38	S. Africa
35	Poland	37	Japan
34	Russia	36	Russia

Trust (60-100)
Neutral (50-59)
Distrust (1-49)

Biggest changes in

U.S.	-9
China	+7
S. Korea	+6
UAE	+6
Italy	-5

Trust decline in the U.S. is the steepest ever measured

Source: Edelman Trust Barometer 2018

One can argue the declines in the 2017 barometer may have been tied to special political factors, such as Brexit, the confusion around the US and Australian elections, the Syrian crisis, and Russia meddling in Ukraine. However, for the declines to continue into 2018 and the drop to be so dramatic, especially in the United States, where the declines were among the largest, was startling. Trust in businesses declined by 10 points in the US, trust in government was down 14 points, and trust in the media by 5 points. In each of these categories, more people said they do not trust these institutions than asserted they do. It's a pretty sad state of affairs for the richest and most powerful country on earth.

Another survey conducted in 2018 by the Reuters Institute for the Study of Journalism asked specifically about trust in news. The survey covered seventy-four thousand online consumers in thirty-seven countries and laid bare our trouble with trust. Only 44 percent said they trusted their news sources. Trust in news found via Google search results was only 34 percent, while trust in news found through social media platforms was an even lower at 23 percent. These declines were linked by the study to three factors: the polarization of the media; the perception of heightened political influence on it; and the desperation of news providers to find revenue streams with the pools of traditional advertising drying up.[3]

Trust has been eroding when it comes to our technology providers. The 2018 Global Survey on Internet Security and Trust, run in twenty-five countries and with 25,262 respondents, showed that consumers have a high level of distrust in social media platforms, search engines and internet technology companies. Sixty-three percent of the respondents said they believed that social media has too much power. Many shared that they are changing their online behavior accordingly, with 12 percent saying they're purchasing less via ecommerce channels, 10 percent reporting they have closed social media accounts, and 8 percent emphasizing they are using the internet less often.

These declines reflect an awareness that the lines between fact and opinion, honesty and deception, real and fake are being increasingly blurred. A new normal is emerging in which opinion and outright fabrications are portrayed as fact. So we are smart to distrust many sources and people in positions of authority. The problem is that the widespread distrust is leading to further polarization, more heated conflict, and denialism.

The post-truth era has given rise to the post-trust era.

We've stopped trusting governments, businesses, and the media the way we once did, and the lack of trust is impairing our ability to address and resolve pressing concerns. Now, one may argue, that the public has never just thrown its trust in our leaders and institutions. But if you zoom out and look at these surveys across a broad stretch of time, the trendlines are consistent - we're nowhere near as trusting as we once were. To begin to tackle this crisis, it helps to understand more about the dynamics of trust. For that, we can turn to social psychologist Morton Deutsch.

THE FATHER OF MODERN-DAY TRUST

Born in Bronx, New York in 1920, Morton Deutsch's parents were Jewish immigrants from what is now Poland. From the start of his life, Deutsch was an extraordinary student, skipping three grades on his way to college. By the age of fifteen, he had enrolled in the City College of New York to better understand what makes human beings tick. Graduating in 1939 at the age of nineteen, Deutsch moved on to receive his master's from the University of Pennsylvania in just one year. Like many of his generation, Deutsch was driven by a sense of duty to join the war after the Pearl Harbor bombing. In 1941, he enrolled in the US Air Force, starting out as a psychologist but later shifting to flying sorties over Nazi Germany. Carrying out more than thirty bombings, he was awarded a Distinguished Flying Cross and an Air Medal.

With the war over, Deutsch revisited his interest in the human condition and went on to pursue his doctorate in social psychology from the Massachusetts Institute of Technology (MIT). Witnessing the horrors of war inspired him to devote the remainder of his life to the cause of peace. Deutsch described his work in social psychology as shadowed by the clouds of atom bombs over Hiroshima and Nagasaki. It was during the period soon after the war that Deutsch made one of his most important contributions to the field of psychology. This contribution is why he is now considered the founder of modern theory and research on trust, and one of the most distinguished psychologists of our time.[4]

Until Deutsch took up the task of analyzing trust, research on the subject had been marred by a lack of precision and consistency in the way the concept was understood. Even today, different cultures have widely disparate definitions of what it actually means to trust. In English, the word trust refers to the belief in the reliability and truth of someone or something. In Norwegian, no noun corresponds to the English definition. In French, the word for trust is construed simply as having confidence in something. In Japanese, a new word was invented merely a century ago to capture the meaning of trust and refers to the belief that someone or something is honest and will not cause harm. Researchers understandably had trouble arriving at a rigorous definition of the term.

Deutsch developed one. He defined trust as the "confidence that [one] will find what is desired [from another] rather than what is feared." He made a core conjecture about the role of trust in well-functioning relationships. If an individual trusts another, he posited, he or she will act cooperatively with that individual. Conversely, if a person doesn't trust another, he or she would behave competitively.[5] To test his theory, Deutsch ran a simple experiment with his graduate students at MIT. Dividing ten students into two groups of five, he gave each a project to do and instructed them to work together. He informed one group they would all share the final grade for the project. The group as a whole would be evaluated on the quality of the final product relative to other groups completing the same exercise, and each of the students in the group would receive the same grade. The second group was given the same assignment, but he explained that each student would be graded separately based on their relative contribution to the final product. The person who contributed the most would get an "A," the person contributing the next most a "B" and so on. Can you guess what happened?

The first group partnered closely, sharing information widely, building on one another's thinking and working collaboratively in a focused way. When conflicts arose within the group, they were able to resolve them quickly and constructively. They worked well together, and their end product was exceptional. Members trusted the intentions of the others in their group and all benefited from doing so.

The second group, on the other hand, was fractious and dysfunctional, bickering and refusing to share information in the greater interest of the group. They were much more concerned with competing against one another than with working together to create a valuable finished product. When conflicts developed, they were unable to recover from them. Those students fared miserably.

Through this study, Deutsch developed his sharpest insights around trust. He argued that trust is the most essential ingredient in the development and maintenance of happy, well-functioning relationships between individuals, groups, and countries. People and societies at large generally work in harmony if trust is the base of their relationship. From business to politics to our social lives, trust develops in relationships in which people work toward mutually beneficial outcomes. Distrust emerges when they are working at cross purposes. People become suspicious of others' intentions, teams compete rather than cooperate, and there is a general breakdown of healthy interactions.

PLAYING THE TRUST GAME

Social scientists have been building on Deutsch's work for decades. One contribution in particular has been used in a host of studies on the dynamics of trust and offers powerful backup for Deutsch's insights. Economists Joyce Berg, John Dickhaut, and Kevin McCabe developed the "Trust Game," which has been the most popular method of measuring trust and trustworthiness. It's easy to play and you could even try it at home with a few friends or family. But beware: it's quite revealing about levels of trust between people.[6]

The game involves two players. Let's call them Jack and Jill. Jack receives an endowment of $10. He then has the choice of how much of that money to send to Jill. He can send anything from none of it to all of it. He is told the money will be tripled on its way to Jill. Thus, the more he sends to Jill, the more money that will ultimately be generated. Jill then has a choice to return as much or as little of the money as she chooses to

Jack. Play this game with different people in your life and you'll probably get different amounts back. The results will vary depending on whether you trust the person at the start of the game.

One of the major findings from studies done with the game is that the more Jack trusts, the more money he sends to Jill, and in turn, the more Jill reciprocates. Researchers believe that Jill returns the money equally split if she feels as though Jack trusted her in the first place. If Jack doesn't initially trust Jill, then Jill is unlikely to feel obligated to return any money and therefore doesn't.

If one's initial degree of trust is the key to outcomes, the logical question that follows is why are so many of us predisposed to distrust one another these days? Deutsch's findings that shared values and mutual incentives are so important provide an answer. Much of what is undermining trust today is that there are such heated value clashes between social groups and many people don't believe they have mutual interests. They therefore choose to act in what they see as their own best interests, or those of their group, rather than serve a collective good. That then further fuels distrust. It's a vicious cycle.

But things don't have to be this way. People are capable of extraordinary amounts of trust given the right conditions. Consider the story of the remarkable bonds of trust in a remote village in India.

A VILLAGE'S OPEN DOORS

The village of Shani Shingnapur, home to roughly four thousand residents, lies a few hundred miles east of the hustle and bustle of Mumbai.

Life in Shani Shingnapur is much like that in any typical Indian village with one striking exception—the entire village has an open-door policy. There are no doors, only door frames, on every house, shop, school and government office. Until very recently, even the village bank had no locks or doors. Cash is stored in unlocked containers, as is jewelry and other precious belongings. The public toilets have no doors, only thin curtains at the entrance for privacy. The same rule applies to the police station which was built in 2015 and also abides by the open-door policy. The villagers are so trusting of one another that even when they leave town, they don't bother to tell their neighbors to watch over their houses in their absence. Villager Ujjwala Dange proudly claims, "There is immense trust within the community and people stick by each other through the toughest of times."[7]

Behind the open-door policy is the deeply held view among the villagers that Lord Shani, the Hindu god of deeds and justice, is watching over and protecting them. The deeply held belief is that Lord Shani would punish anyone who attempted a crime. But the villagers have another reason to trust one another. The village has become famous for its open doors, and roughly forty thousand visitors flock to it everyday to pay homage to Lord Shani. This gives villagers a strong incentive to trust one another as well as trust in Lord Shani. The village economy thrives due to all of the visitors, which is in everyone's interest. If people started installing doors, the village would lose its mystique and the flood of visitors would likely become a trickle.

How does a society like this exist? And why aren't there more acts of deviance in the village? One would assume that less security would yield higher crime and corruption. Skeptics say the remoteness of the village is probably a greater influence than protection by a god. However, there are thousands of remote villages across India, yet none have an open-door policy. There's something else at play. Per Deutsch's findings, the villagers have both their shared religious values and their strong mutual economic interests to bolster their trust.

Now let's consider another community in which initial trust has been eroded to its potential great peril. We need to look no further than the ongoing travails of Facebook to see the corrosive effects on trust if people begin to believe that the platform doesn't share their values and have mutual interests.

TRUSTING FACEBOOK TODAY

Facebook has approximately 1.5 billion daily active users and 2.2 billion monthly active users in a world of 7.4 billion people. That's even before you begin counting users of the company's other important platforms WhatsApp and Instagram, which also number in the billions. With all these users, the Facebook stock price has seen astronomical growth over the last few years as has its market capitalization. That all changed on March 19, 2018, when the Facebook stock price dropped an astonishing 7 percent in the span of twenty-four hours. The next day was nearly as bad. Over those two trading sessions, almost $50 billion in market capitalization was wiped out. What caused the dramatic drop? It boiled down to a matter of trust.

In case you haven't followed the story closely in the news, here's how the Facebook saga began. In 2013, a university researcher collected data from 270,000 Facebook users. Back then, Facebook cavalierly allowed third parties to collect data from users and their friends. That meant that the researcher was able to collect data on the friends of those users as well. The researcher ended up acquiring data on 87 million Facebook users without having to ask for their explicit permission. At the time, this was all perfectly legal. A year later, that researcher shared the data with Cambridge Analytica, a UK marketing firm hired by the Trump campaign. The firm then used the data to create user profiles against which highly targeted advertising was run to further the agendas of politicians running for government. While the way the data was extracted from Facebook was legal, the manner in which it was used to create user profiles and run targeted advertising by a third party violated Facebook policies and US law. So, while Facebook hadn't technically broken the law in any way itself, the policies of the platform at the time of the data harvesting provided fertile ground for the stealing to take place and for a major national election to have been meddled with.[8]

It wasn't just the stock market that reacted with horror. A number of companies temporarily pulled their advertising from Facebook. Tesla CEO Elon Musk and celebrities Will Ferrell, Susan Sarandon, Jim Carrey, and Cher (to name a few) joined the #DeleteFacebook movement. Thousands of users signed a petition demanding that Facebook provide better protection of their data.

The weekend the news first broke, Shoptalk, the largest retail conference in America, was underway. On stage being interviewed by a CNBC anchor was the vice president of global marketing solutions at Facebook. The first five questions were about the data scandal that was unfolding in real time. The Facebook VP said that the company was "outraged and beyond disturbed," and it was quickly obvious from the following answers that the folks at Facebook were shaking in their boots. And this was before the stock markets had opened and the share price had begun to plummet. Even though the company had broken no laws, so didn't have to worry about being prosecuted or fined for malfeasance, Facebook leadership understood the gravity of the situation: that users' trust had been violated.[9]

Over the years, users had exposed so much of their personal lives on the platform, with the belief that only their friends would be privy to it. Once Facebook started advertising, users generally understood that their data was being used to target ads to them, but that seemed a mutually beneficial arrangement. Facebook continued to provide users with more and more wonderful features and users enabled Facebook to achieve great earnings. The key, though, was that users thought that whatever information they shared would only be used, in some anonymous form, to help target more relevant ads that also could be beneficial to them. Some of the ads could actually be appealing and make for convenient purchasing. The fact that the data had been taken from Facebook, sold to third parties and then used to manipulate them was a blatant violation of the understanding of mutual benefits. Facebook had not protected them against this breach of data, and users were left wondering whether their privacy was really much of a concern for the company. To users, Facebook seemed only to care about building its ad revenue and had fallen down on the job of privacy protection, whether wittingly or not. In Deutsch's framework, users had less confidence that their association with Facebook was built on shared values and a constructive, cooperative relationship with mutual incentives in which both parties gained. It appeared that only Cambridge Analytica was gaining in this scenario, and at their expense.

That's why Facebook was so concerned and why they've worked tirelessly since then to rebuild the public's trust. The company's leaders understood another of Morton Deutsch's key insights—while trust is difficult to build, it is relatively easy to destroy.

Hindsight is 20/20, and it's easy to look back and see how and where Facebook went wrong. They immediately went to work strengthening their data controls. Steps were taken to change their data usage policies; more aggressively scrutinize third parties who partner with them; limit how user data can be manipulated; and further educate consumers, developers, regulators and business partners on how piracy works on the platform. In an effort to limit fake news, in October 2018, Facebook removed eight hundred pages and accounts that, in its words, violated its rules "against spam and coordinated inauthentic behavior."[10] But fortifying the walls where data had leaked is only part of the solution. And the much easier part at that. Rebuilding user trust is the other part.

Facebook has since launched a massive advertising campaign in an attempt to reassure users they could once again trust the platform. The ad starts by reminding people why they initially joined Facebook, and then pledges "Facebook will do more to keep you safe and protect your privacy, so we can all get back to what made Facebook great in the first place: friends." After all, if you can't trust your friends, whom can you trust?

The Facebook saga is still unfolding as we write this. CEO Mark Zuckerberg has rightfully stated that "If we're going to achieve what we want to, it's not about the best features. It's about building the best community." The entire business of Facebook is built on the premise that people will share their lives with their friends. If they stop, Facebook will become nothing more than a ghost town. These words of Abraham Lincoln come to mind, "If you once forfeit the confidence of your fellow citizens, you can never regain their respect and esteem."

Working in Facebook's favor is the fact that it did not intend for user data to be sold to a nefarious third-party, and it made no money itself from the sales. It had no interest in Cambridge Analytica's success and every interest in the firm's subsequent demise. In this instance, the interests of the trusted and the trusters actually were in agreement. Facebook does have a huge stake in privacy protection, which it has gotten a jolting wake-up call about. It now has to convincingly show that it values that protection.

This story highlights that knowing whom and what to trust, and when, is far from a clear black-and-white issue. Given that user trust is the bedrock of Facebook's success, it wasn't unreasonable to expect the company to be extremely vigilant about privacy. Which leads us to one last feature of trust to emphasize—it almost always involves some leap of faith.

TRUST IS RISKY BUSINESS

Deutsch's work turned trust into a hot research topic in a wide range of disciplines. From politics to management, psychology, economics, healthcare, and ethics, trust became all the rage. It has become one of the most popular and trendy buzzwords over the last fifty years. While competing definitions have been promoted, there is a common thread that ties most together. The commonality is that trust inherently requires us to accept vulnerability. Colloquially, we know this as 'taking a leap of faith.'

A willingness to take a risk is present in all trust situations. This is because it's generally impossible to know fully what "the truth" is, even without all of the frenzy of deception currently going on. We have limited information regarding almost any situation we are involved in and every decision we make. It's not practical for us to test the contents of every product we purchase, or to look up the string of facts that would be needed to verify every claim we hear a pundit make. This is also another way the technology boom has challenged us.

Using new technologies almost always requires what Rachel Botsman, author of *Who Can You Trust?: How Technology Brought Us Together and Why It Might Drive Us Apart,* calls *trust leaps.*[11] Think of the first time you entered your credit card details into an internet site, ordered an item off of eBay, or shared a ride on Uber. Those were all trust leaps. So now the question becomes, how do we make the best judgment calls? How do we do the best job we can of adjudicating when to make a trust leap and when not to? Psychology has provided a set of powerful insights that we can use. Research has revealed how differently individuals perceive situations and evaluate information, uncovering a set of cognitive biases that color our perceptions of events, information, and people. Becoming mindful of them can help us stay alert and ask ourselves important questions about how we're thinking and feeling about any given claim so as to prevent becoming a victim of deception.

But before moving on to that terrain, pause to consider what Deutsch's research on trust teaches us about strengthening the bonds of trust in our lives. Think about every relationship you have, whether it be with the leaders at your company, the publications you turn to for your news, or your friends and family. Ask yourself, are their interests in alignment with yours and are they truly incented to help you succeed as much as you may be vested in their success? Are you contributing enough to develop a more trusting relationship with them? Are you investing in the relationship, making some trust leaps? Alternatively, are you perhaps trusting in some people and news sources that you should be more skeptical of?

Keep revisiting these questions as you read the following chapters. While knowing whom, what, and when to trust has become more difficult than ever, trust is still the essential binding agent of all good relationships, and of a well-functioning society. It's the key to a happy marriage, strong friendships, successful community building, political problem-solving, and thriving in business. Research from three different countries that surveyed 7,700 work teams discovered that higher team trust yields better team performance.[12] Another study surveyed 12,750 workers across various industries and found that highly trusting organizations had a total return to shareholders that was 286 percent higher than companies that scored low on trust.[13]

We all have great stakes in knowing how to cultivate trust and combat fakery. The very foundation of becoming savvy about trust is appreciating that we are all unfortunately subject to biases that both color our perceptions and lead us, often unconsciously, to buy into and even perpetuate fakeness.

GET SAVVY NOW
OVERCOMING OUR CRISIS IN TRUST

- **Give more trust to get more trust:** If you want to build trust, take the initiative to create a trusted environment. Give more early on. It will increase the likelihood of the trust being reciprocated. The more you trust a person, the more likely are they to return that trust exponentially.

- **Create shared, mutual goals:** When establishing trusted relationships with others, focus on developing shared goals. Make sure that your objectives and the other person's objectives are aligned. Have conversations to better understand each other's goals.

- **Take responsibility to rebound:** Mistakes are inevitable but can be an opportunity for growth. Take responsibility for the role you played in breaking the trust and clearly articulate your plan to rebuild it. Present action items and work steadfastly to deliver them.

- **Create a culture of transparency:** In creating a relationship built on trust, it is important to be as open and honest as possible. Be able to articulate your mission as well as the challenges that you face in achieving it.

- **Handle with care:** Given that trust is difficult to build and easy to destroy, always handle it with care. What may take years to establish, can be undone in minutes.

CHAPTER 2

● ● ● ● ●

WE FALL FOR
ALTERNATIVE FACTS

"It's not a matter of what is true that counts, but a matter of
what is perceived to be true."

— HENRY KISSINGER

INAUGURATION CROWDS

PRESIDENT TRUMP WAS INAUGURATED ON FRIDAY, JANUARY 20, 2017.
The next day, White House Press Secretary, Sean Spicer, at his very first
press conference declared that the crowd "was the largest audience ever
to witness an inauguration, period, both in person and around the globe."
He was implicitly drawing a comparison between Trump's inauguration and former president Obama's. However, a side-by-side comparison
of video footage from the two inaugurations clearly showed that more
people were present at Obama's inauguration.[1] According to Nielsen

ratings (the audience measurement system), both Reagan and Obama also had significantly more viewers on TV during their inaugurations in 1981 and 2008 than Trump.[2]

Even after much criticism in the press and online about Spicer's comments, Kellyanne Conway, advisor to President Trump, adamantly defended him during a Meet the Press interview the following day. Conway explained that Spicer had simply given the media "alternative facts." Host Chuck Todd interrupted her, saying, "Wait a minute. Alternative facts? ... Look, alternative facts are not facts. They're falsehoods." Conway disagreed, and we'd crossed yet another line, it seemed, in the advance of post-truth.[3]

For every news item these day, facts and alternative facts are presented. Some of the deception is hard to detect. But how could it be that when shown indisputable evidence of a falsehood, some people nevertheless choose to believe it? How could anyone in their right mind look at that video footage and not concede the truth? More likely than not, those people actually do see the differences in the video footage, but believe that those images themselves are doctored and fake. So they create a narrative for themselves that allows them to logically believe what they want. Certainly some of the unabashed support for false claims is simple disingenuousness. People know the truth but refuse to admit it because they see denying it as in their interest. But it's very hard to know when this is the case because people also subscribe to falsehoods out of irrationality.

We all have subconscious motivations to believe untrustworthy news, arguments, and people. We want to believe that, for the most part, we are logical beings, but the stark reality is we are constantly under the influence of cognitive biases that distort our perception and sway our judgments. The variance in how different people perceive and interpret any given piece of news or event they experience can be truly mind-boggling. Take the case of one recent tragedy that provoked wildly divergent interpretations.

ONE EVENT, MANY VIEWS

Danielle Gilbert was discussing Freud in her AP Psychology class a little after 2:35 p.m. on a warm, sunny day. Suddenly, she heard gunshots and watched as the glass in her classroom door exploded and flew in every direction. The room filled with dust and debris and people began to shriek in terror. As Danielle recalled, "Once I stopped hearing shots, I stood up to see why those students were making so much noise and what I saw at that moment will haunt me for the rest of my life. I saw my classmates, my friends, people I knew so well, laying on the floor, covered in blood completely lifeless."[4]

A few minutes earlier, Nikolas Cruz had stepped out of an Uber and walked toward building 12, a three-story structure that housed thirty classrooms and some nine hundred students, of Stoneman Douglas High School in Parkland, Florida. Cruz entered the building, pulled the fire alarm, wielded an AR-15 semi-automatic rifle and started firing indiscriminately at students and teachers. Six minutes and twenty seconds later, fourteen students and three staff members lay dead while seventeen others had sustained non-fatal injuries.

In the wake of the shooting, a myriad of narratives of what happened and who was to blame unfolded. Instead of coming together as a country, America splintered apart. Instead of joining arms and mourning, people quickly moved to accusations, falsifications and revisionism. Many people were unwilling to trust information that contradicted their world view. People privileged whatever facts, alternative facts, or exaggerations supported their opinions and chose their preferred parties to blame. This was, in part, because they genuinely saw the event differently, which becomes apparent if we look at the tragedy from their various perspectives.

Let's begin with Emma González. A senior at Stoneman Douglas High School, González was in the auditorium with several others when the fire alarm went off. She tried to leave the building but was instructed to take cover. She and others were held in the auditorium for two hours until police eventually released them. A week after the shooting, she participated in a Fort Lauderdale protest condemning the tragedy and lack of gun regulation in America. She famously proclaimed, "We call BS" on the apathy of politicians funded by the National Rifle Association (NRA) who refused to moderate gun laws enforcing stricter background checks. She believed such legislation could have prevented the shooting, and her focus was on the inaction of political leaders at the national, state, and county levels. A few weeks later, at the March for Our Lives demonstration in Washington DC (the largest student rally in American history) González asked the crowd of approximately eight hundred thousand to join her in a full six minutes of silence—the amount of time Cruz had roamed the school during his rampage. She wanted people to imagine how it felt to be hiding in silence, terrified of being shot. This has since been dubbed the "loudest silence" in the history of US social protest.[5]

Scot Peterson, a Broward County school resource officer, controversially experienced the shooting from outside the building. At the time of the shooting, the school had eight security guards, seven of whom were unarmed, limiting their ability to move against Cruz. Peterson was the eighth guard and carried a gun, and he's been blamed for staying outside. His initial explanation was that he'd mistaken the shooting for firecrackers. Once he recognized it was rifle fire, he alerted his superiors and then searched for a safe spot where he waited until the shooting subsided. According to Peterson, he did everything that his training asked of him, calling in the shooting, putting the school on lockdown and ushering kids out of harm's way. He has since steadfastly maintained that he fulfilled his job requirements.[6]

Several of the victim's family members saw Peterson's behavior very differently. Philip Schentrup, whose daughter Carmen died in the shooting, called Peterson, a "coward and a liar" going on to say, "He is attempting to create a narrative about him as a victim instead of the truth." Andrew Pollack, whose daughter Meadow also died in the shooting, argued that Peterson should have been fired four years earlier for undue leniency in a case of bullying. Peterson had let the bullies off easy, Pollack said, because one of them was the local sheriff's son. Peterson's direct boss was that sheriff. Had Peterson been fired at that time, a more competent guard may have prevented the Parkland tragedy four years later. Pollack asserted that Peterson didn't take his job seriously enough on that fateful day because he knew the sheriff would protect him in the end.[7]

The media crafted several other narratives of their own, which were of course vastly different. The right wing alternative media quickly got to work spinning the story as almost anything but an access to guns issue. Conservative media pundits blamed the school administration, Cruz's parents, lack of Christian values, and even the students themselves. Some from the far right signaled their support for conspiracy theories claiming the students were crisis actors trained in victim behavior as a way to further their political agenda. Less than a week after the event, more than one hundred thousand Facebook users had shared a post asserting that the Parkland students were crisis actors.[8]

Some members of the right-wing media also attempted to alter the conversation to deflect from the tragedy of the shooting. Laura Ingraham, a Fox News primetime anchor and NRA supporter, made a conscious decision to denigrate David Hogg, another of the Stoneman Douglas School survivors. Tweeting to her 2.4 million followers, Ingraham criticized Hogg's inability to gain admission to certain US colleges, then linked to an article calling him a "gun rights provocateur." She used her microphone to deflect from the tragedy and mock a survivor—all in an attempt to stand in good stead with the NRA and her more conservative viewers. Advertisers found her behavior shocking and started to withdraw their ads from her show. But Ingraham wasn't just one rogue talk show host attempting to alter the narrative.[9]

Other conservative media outlets put their focus on the liberal media. Sinclair Broadcasting, which owns a network of 193 local television stations through which it reaches 40 percent of American households, sent a message from its headquarters in Maryland shortly after the shooting to each of its local affiliates mandating that they read a message on air. The message included a grave warning about fake news and what national broadcasters may or may not be saying. While the message didn't explicitly mention the tragedy, the subtext was clear: don't believe the liberal media and its spin-doctoring around gun control. Deadspin composed a video clip showing the anchors of all the affiliates repeating the message verbatim, causing an uproar. The anchors came across as robots, suspending their editorial judgment and parroting a corporate message whether they agreed or not.[10]

On the flip side, the liberal media machines also got to work generating their own slant. The narrative they endorsed blamed politicians for lax gun laws, the NRA for funding the politicians in exchange for support, and the general gun culture of middle America. Some liberal outlets called for the Second Amendment to be repealed, declaring it outdated. They argued that when it was adopted in 1791 there were no weapons like the AR-15 assault rifle and that citizens didn't have access to firearms in nearly the same way as they do today.[11]

Then there was the outright fake news. A few days after the March for Our Lives demonstration, Teen Vogue interviewed González and uploaded a photograph of her tearing up a gun target poster. The photograph, which spread rapidly to other social media platforms, had been doctored by Gab, a "free speech network." The doctored photo showed her tearing up a copy of the US Constitution instead of the gun target poster. Dark circles were added under González's eyes and she was made to look sinister.[12] Through the sheer speed of its distribution, the photo gained legitimacy. Suddenly, it had become fact and we had yet another narrative (and another example of what it's like to live in the post-trust era).

A number of politicians wove their own distortions. Senator Marco Rubio, in particular, knew that much of the nation was pointing the finger at him. Just two years earlier, the NRA had given over $1 million to his reelection campaign. Rubio quickly tried to position himself as pushing for compromise on gun control legislation. He commiserated with the students at a CNN town hall in Florida that was filmed for a national audience and proffered support for a law that would prevent eighteen year-olds from buying a rifle, unequivocally proclaiming, "I will support a law that takes that right away."[13] Roughly a thousand miles away in Washington, DC, however, Rubio continued to lead a Senate campaign to overturn a law that already banned eighteen year olds from buying a rifle. Even after the contradiction was highlighted, Rubio refused to retract his sponsorship of the bill, excusing his stance by saying he was trying to bring District of Columbia law in line with Federal law. Many believe that Rubio's interest in DC local matters had more to do with the fact that he had received approximately $3.3 million in direct and indirect contributions from the NRA and its supporters over the course of his career (and hoped to continue receiving those funds into the future).[14]

Then there's President Trump. The narrative he stood behind placed part of the blame on the student survivors, stating, "So many signs that the Florida shooter was mentally disturbed, even expelled from school for erratic behavior. Neighbors and classmates knew he was a big problem. Must always report such instances to authorities, again and again!"[15] He also pointed his finger at the FBI, tweeting three days after the shooting, "Very sad that the FBI missed all of the many signals sent out by the Florida school shooter. This is not acceptable. They are spending too much time trying to prove Russian collusion with the Trump campaign—there is no collusion. Get back to the basics and make us all proud!"[16]

Most companies responded with a deafening silence. Tragedies were difficult for companies as it was always too easy to come across as opportunistic in a time of sorrow. Political battles in the Trump era were even more dangerous for companies to wade into as they risked alienating customers. However, there were a few exceptions—companies who made statements through the actions they took in response to the tragedy. Soon after the shooting, Dick's Sporting Goods, one of America's largest sporting goods and gun retailers, announced that it would stop selling assault rifles. Though it wasn't the gun used in the Parkland shooting, Nicholas Cruz had bought a weapon from Dick's Sporting Goods the previous November. In announcing the decision, the CEO of Dick's Sporting Goods, Edward Stack said, "We recognize and appreciate that the vast majority of gun owners in this country are responsible, law-abiding citizens. But we have to help solve the problem that's in front of us."[17] United, Delta, Hertz, Alamo, and MetLife also took strong positions by ending their partnerships with the NRA in the aftermath of the tragedy.

The horrific shooting of seventeen innocent people in Parkland was seen, and explained, through so many different lenses, and subject to so much partisan spin, that no one narrative prevailed. But one thing about the tragedy is blindingly clear: the "truth" was in the eye of the beholder. And this "truth" is distorted by preconceptions, self-interest, and fealty to one or another group.

One's view of what is true is always distorted by the psychological biases of both the spinners and the spun, in all walks of life. What any one of us sees as the simple truth is almost always in fact a biased narrative. Even in cases when it would seem that eventually getting down to the facts of the matter is inevitable, that, as the saying goes, the truth will out, the truth will actually often remain in dispute. For every fact, there may continue to be an alternative fact. This is not only true for America either.

LEE JAE-YONG DID NOTHING WRONG

Lee Jae-yong is worth $6 billion. He's the grandson of Samsung founder Lee Byung-chul and the son of the current chairman Lee Kun-hee. Holding a degree from South Korea's top university, a doctorate from Harvard Business School, and several years of growing responsibility within Samsung, he's been groomed his entire life to take over the family firm. With approximately $300 billion in annual revenue and 490,000 employees, Samsung is the largest conglomerate in South Korea, responsible for 20 percent of the country's economy. It is also one of the largest global technology companies. According to *Forbes* magazine, Lee was ranked the 40th most powerful person in the world—until February 2017.

On February 17 of that year, Lee was arrested and charged over his alleged role in a political and corporate scandal that captivated all of South Korea and led to the eventual downfall of its president, Park Geun-hye. Lee was put on trial for bribery and embezzlement, which included making payments of $36 million to two non-profit foundations operated by Choi Soon-sil, Park's close friend, in exchange for political support. Favors rendered included backing a controversial Samsung merger which paved the way for Lee to eventually become head of the conglomerate. The deal needed support from the government-run national pension fund.[18]

Lee denied the charges. While he admitted to making the donations, he explained that he had neither wanted nor expected anything in return. He wrote a letter to the court, his employees, the press, and the public at large apologizing for the mess but refusing to take any blame. Meanwhile, the 200-person corporate strategy team at Samsung, which dictated the group's overall direction and major business decisions, was disbanded and a former vice-chairman of the group, Choi Gee-sung (who ran the unit) assumed all the blame. In his testimony, Choi stated, "Final approvals for most business decisions at the group were made by me, under my responsibility," adding he did not tell Lee about the payments. But in August 2017, Lee was convicted and sentenced to five years in prison. End of the story? Far from it.[19]

Despite many hours of testimony and voluminous document discovery, Lee's guilt has remained contested. His lawyers appealed the case, and in February of 2018, the Seoul High Court first reduced Lee's sentence by half and then later let him walk free.

Did he commit a crime? We don't know. He could have been innocent. That's still the multi-billion-dollar question swirling around the country. Some people in South Korea are adamant that he is guilty, while others are staunch believers in his innocence. Many in the general public, which was already suspicious of Samsung's cozy ties with the government, were appalled by his release. Those affiliated in some way with Samsung saw the case very differently.[20] Employees, investors, and suppliers have largely expressed their support of Lee and argued the judiciary was out to get him. His customers don't seem too concerned either, as the company reported record profits by the spring of 2018.

Such vast divides in belief about the truth concerning even issues of major national importance are dangerous to the healthy functioning of society. If our biases prevent us from finding common ground when even the most fundamental principles of accountability and justice are concerned, we are on a windy road toward dysfunction. The epidemic of alternative facts is so troubling because it is deepening divisions by playing on our natural biases.

In order to combat the manipulation of our perceptions and views by the purveyors of fakery, we have to understand how our biases operate. We also have to understand that the same biases are imprinted in us all. Why? Because through the course of early human evolution, when the fundamental nature of our minds was fixed, they were adaptive. They are thought to have played some role in helping us survive. But they're quite crude mechanisms, and often more harmful than helpful to us in modern life. They lead to impulsive decisions, willful blindness, and make us astonishingly gullible. To begin investigating the specific ways in which our biases make us vulnerable to manipulation, let's consider one of the most blatant ways we can be fooled.

REPETITION MAKES THE TRUTH

Have you noticed how political campaigns are run? Take any major democracy across the world and you will notice some striking similarities in how political campaigns transpire. The candidate is presented as a story in perfection—crafted to fit a particular image that voters may have in their minds. He or she is trustworthy, ambitious, patriotic, caring, family-oriented, strong but empathetic, and willing and able to understand (and fix!) the ordinary person's concerns. Regardless of whether the candidate is on the left or right of the political spectrum, he or she is introduced in a similar fashion, with the same traits and accomplishments being accentuated. And for the rest of the campaign, every major political speech, every advertisement, every event, and every debate is staged to reinforce that core message. The tactic works quite well because one of the glitches built into the human mind is that repetition leads people to believe a message. It is in fact, one of the easiest methods of persuasion. This phenomenon is called the illusory truth effect. Accounts of it go back to the early days of the Roman Empire and the Punic Wars.

The Punic Wars were a series of three wars fought between Rome and Carthage from 264 BC to 146 BC. At the time, they were some of the largest wars to have ever taken place. As the Roman Republic grew in influence and military strength, it kept knocking against the Carthaginian (Punic) Empire, the dominant western Mediterranean maritime empire based out of modern-day Tunisia. The Romans and Carthaginians fought for trading influence and land. Rome won the first war.

The second Punic War was won by the Romans after Hannibal (Carthage's leader) crossed the Alps, entered Italy via the north, and then got bogged down in mainland Italy without a clear endgame in sight. He was stuck for sixteen years in the Italian countryside making vain attempts to take the city of Rome only to be thwarted again and again. Eventually, with supplies dwindling, threats to his homebase in Northern Africa, and his army tired, Hannibal retreated home, where at the Battle of Zama, he was eventually defeated. This was the end to the second Punic War. Carthage had lost approximately 20,000 troops with an additional 15,000 wounded. In comparison, the Romans suffered only 2,500 casualties.

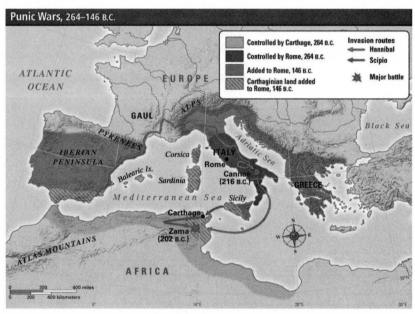

Source: worldhistory88.wordpress.com

Under the terms of the treaty, the Carthaginians were not allowed to maintain an army and had to pay an indemnity. However, there was significant improvement in Carthaginian wealth and martial power in the fifty years since the second Punic War, creating even more animosity among the Romans. They vied for dominance over the seafaring and prosperous Phoenician city-state of Carthage and suffered a series of humiliations and damaging reverses during smaller confrontations after the second Punic War. Romans may have won the first two Punic Wars, but Carthage continued to needle them and stir agitation in the streets of Rome.

That was when one Roman senator, Cato the Elder, took to ending his speeches in the senate with the expression, "Carthago delenda est" which loosely translates to "Carthage must be destroyed." He did this even in speeches that were completely unrelated to Roman foreign policy toward Carthage. Cato closed his speeches with a call to destroy Carthage because he knew that repetition of the sentiment would eventually breed agreement in the senate. And lo and behold it did. He was practicing the illusory truth effect well before the principle even had a name![21]

A much more recent example of the illusory truth effect comes to us from Donald Trump's 2015 presidential campaign. Over the course of various debates and interviews, Trump repeatedly echoed the phrase, "Crooked Hillary." Among his accusations, Trump claimed that Hillary Clinton had ties to Wall Street, used her private email server to send government-related messages, had conflicts of interest with the Clinton Foundation, and was responsible for the security lapses resulting in the 2012 attack on the US diplomatic compound in Benghazi. A Politi-Fact survey showed that a whopping 70 percent of Trump's statements during the campaign were false. Meanwhile, just 26 percent of Hillary's were deemed false.[22] And yet, Trump was successful in convincing large segments of the population that Hillary was indeed the "crooked" one.

The illusory truth effect was given its name in a 1977 study by Villanova University and Temple University researchers Lynn Hasher, David Goldstein, and Thomas Toppino.[23] For the study, volunteers rated a series of trivia questions as either true or false. Hours, weeks, even months later, the experimenters brought the subjects back for a quiz. Some of the statements on the quiz were new and some were repeats from the original quiz. Time and again, people rated statements they'd seen before as being true regardless of whether or not they were. The researchers argue that familiar statements are easier to process relative to novel, unknown statements. And so, when assessing whether a statement is true, people unconsciously choose to rely on information that sounds like something they've heard before.

More recently, psychologists Gordon Pennycook and David Rand examined the illusory truth effect using experiments with fake news headlines from the 2016 US presidential campaign.[24] Participants in their study were shown an equal number of fake and real headlines and then asked how accurate they were. An example of a fake news headline was a picture of Mike Pence with the caption, "Gay conversion saved my marriage." A sample of a real news headline was a picture of Vladimir Putin with the caption "Vladimir Putin 'personally involved' in US hack, report claims." After judging whether the headlines were real or fake, participants were distracted with another task for a while. They were then given a list of twenty-four headlines to evaluate, which included all of the headlines they had seen previously, as well as a set of completely new (real and fake) headlines.

The results showed that when participants had previously been exposed to a fake news headline they were more likely to accept it as truth later on. *Every* time a lie is repeated, it is slightly more believable to most people. For example, the headline "Trump to Ban All TV Shows that Promote Gay Activity Starting with Empire…" was only rated as accurate by 5 percent of subjects in Pennycook's study. A single prior exposure to that headline doubled the number of participants rating it as true.

Repetition is a key tool that managers across all industries use to drive their message home. Management journals have consistently concluded that employees act on a message only after they've heard executives repeat it multiple times. The next time you're walking down the corridors of a major corporation or government office, pay attention to the signage on the walls. You'll notice the same signs appear many times over. And the messages from those signs were probably explained in company town halls, shared via company email distribution lists, and highlighted on the company intranet. An analysis of Fortune 500 company annual reports and quarterly earnings press releases would certainly also reveal plenty of repetition. Business leaders know that a single exposure to a message is nowhere near enough. Psychologists have studied this phenomenon more closely and found that a message needs to be repeated between ten and twenty times for maximum buy-in. After that point, preference turns into annoyance.

We all know perfectly well that simply hearing something over and over again doesn't mean it is truth, but we fall for this persuasive tactic anyway. Why? This would seem to be a matter of pure mental dysfunction, but if we dig deeper into the psychology behind this, we'll see that the illusory truth effect is a symptom of a bias we have toward things that are familiar to us. The more often we hear something, the more familiar it becomes, and familiarity breeds trust.

There was, and still is, a certain logic to this. Putting our trust in situations, things, and people we were familiar with is thought to have been a good survival tactic in the era before we were fully evolved. We roamed around in small tribes, vulnerable to many dangers, including other tribes we might encounter at any moment. Trusting those in our group and bonding deeply with them was key to making our way through the challenges. The problem is that our minds now over-rely on it.

OUR DANGEROUS COMFORT WITH FAMILIARITY

The familiarity bias leads us to reflexively put more trust in people and their claims simply because they are familiar to us. The effect has been demonstrated clearly in research, such as in an interesting study by psychologist Lisa DeBruine.[25]

DeBruine had volunteers play the Trust Game (which we highlighted in the first chapter), with a couple of twists. One was instead of playing the game in person, the subjects played it over the internet. The other variation involved only one person playing the game. The subject was shown a picture of who they were ostensibly playing against on a monitor. In reality, all of the "partner responses" were computer-generated. In each round, the subject played against one of sixteen possible partners. All of the faces were "morphs"—that either combined the subject's face with the face of a stranger or combined the faces of two strangers. Time and time again, people were much more likely to trust their partner when the partner's image resembled their own. This familiarity bias all too often leads to racial, ethnic, or gender discrimination, that while often unconscious, can do great harm and make us vulnerable to alternative facts.

Just how out-of-step with the conditions of contemporary life this bias is can be seen in studies of the great value of diversity in a workforce. A McKinsey study from January 2018 showed that ethnic and cultural diversity is directly correlated with profitability in Brazil, Mexico, Singapore, South Africa, United Kingdom, and the United States (these are the countries for which they were able to gather data).[26] Companies with the most ethnically diverse executive teams, in both absolute representation and mix of ethnicities, were 33 percent more likely to outperform their peers on profitability. The McKinsey research also demonstrated that executive teams of outperforming companies have more women in line roles versus staff roles. Specifically, having gender diversity on the executive teams was positively correlated with higher profitability.

Trust built on a bias of familiarity limits our ability to make the best decisions. We either close our minds to the information and insight we could draw on from those we don't feel as comfortable with, or we over-rely on those whose experience and views are similar to ours. It also makes us more receptive to alternative facts presented by those we feel simpatico with. We often even trust them when they're making absurdly extreme negative characterizations of people and their behavior, as so many people did with Trump's portrayal of "Crooked Hillary." Not to mention a host of bizarre conspiracy theories about her. Some people even believed she was running a child pornography operation out of a pizzeria in Washington, a nugget of wildly brazen fake news that nonetheless tore around the web.

Negative characterizations of candidates are, of course, the sine qua non of political campaigns. The negative far outweighs the positive in politicking, even with so much criticism through the years of negative campaigning. Why? Because it works. Why is that? Because the negative also far outweighs positive in our minds, another of the well-documented cognitive biases that plague us.

WE'D RATHER BE NEGATIVE

A wealth of studies have shown that we have a tendency to put more trust in negative statements than positive ones. That's true with political campaigns even though we're well aware that campaigns have a long history of deception and a vested interest in tearing their opponents down. We know they are grossly exaggerated, and yet they sway us anyway.

One of the researchers who has documented this bias is psychologist John Cacioppo at Ohio State University. He presented people with pictures known to arouse positive feelings (e.g., a Ferrari, pizza), negative feelings (e.g., a mutilated face, a dead cat), or neutral feelings (e.g., a plate, a hairdryer). As he presented the images, he recorded their brain's electrical activity, reflecting the magnitude of information processing taking place. Cacioppo found that the brain reacts more strongly to stimuli it perceives as negative. In turn, our attitudes are more heavily influenced by negative information than positive information.[27]

Psychologist Daniel Kahneman also revealed this bias when he asked participants to imagine losing or gaining $50.[28] He found that people had a much greater reaction to the prospect of losing the money than to that of gaining it. The bottom line: the mind reacts to bad things more powerfully than it does to equivalent good things. Bad things may be less factual, but we lean into them more anyway.

The negativity bias seems not only irrational but flat-out self-defeating. Wouldn't life be more pleasant if we emphasized the good in it more than the bad? Indeed, there is a wealth of research attesting to the power of positive thinking. So why are we so bad at it? The negativity bias originally developed as an adaptive mechanism. Giving more heed to negative information than positive is thought to have been useful in keeping us out of harm's way. Daily survival depended on shirking dangerous situations, so our brains developed systems to make us ultra-sensitive to possible threats, which allowed us to respond quickly.

This bias helps explain another challenging aspect of the dynamics of trust—how quickly it can be lost. As a Dutch saying goes, "Trust comes on foot but leaves on horseback." Most often, we build trusted relationships over time, methodically banking positive experiences. But in part because our minds are skewed to assign greater weight to negative information than positive information, one or two violations of trust can fatally undermine even a long-established relationship. This is another good reason for Facebook to work furiously to get its privacy house in order; otherwise it might well become a house of cards.

OUR BIASES DO NOT YIELD READILY

It's encouraging that when it comes to alternative facts, some great efforts are underway to catch them as they spread and expose the fakery behind them to the public. Websites like FactCheck.org, PolitiFact, and Snopes receive millions of visitors each month from people seeking to evaluate the accuracy of various claims. But unfortunately, due to the strength of our cognitive biases, mere fact-checking won't be enough to turn the tide of fakeness. Presenting people with well-researched, impartial information is not a sufficient means of convincing them of the truth. Consider what happened to Snopes when it was engaged to fact-check items by Facebook.

Until recently, Snopes was headquartered in San Diego, in a non-descript strip mall, with offices appearing as if they're designed to underwhelm. That's how the founders wanted it; they weren't looking for huge revenue growth or flashy press—they had a simple mission: to be a go-to website for journalists fact-checking urban legends and news. The site was started in 1994 with a focus on fact-checking wide-spread myths in popular culture. David Mikkelson created Snopes to be the "go to place for Internet users to query about anything question-able they encountered online." Recent popular queries include "Did President Trump Incorrectly Color the American Flag?" (unproven) and "Does a New Facebook Algorithm Only Show You 26 Friends?" (false). Since its inception, Snopes has grown due to the surge of fake news. Each month, around 30 million people visit the website to do their own fact checking.

Then along came the 2016 US presidential election, which catapulted the site to notoriety. It was suddenly in the eye of the political storm, with fact checkers and counter fact checkers using the platform to verify claims made by candidates and the media. Brooke Binkowski, Snopes' managing editor at the time, sharply commented, "Rationality seems to have fallen out of vogue. People don't know what to believe anymore. Everything is really strange right now."[29] Until then, Snopes was widely seen as an impartial observer, but things were about to change.

In the aftermath of the election and through 2017, people started accusing Facebook of allowing fake news to spread through its social networking platform. In an effort to blunt some of the criticism and promote only truth-based news, Facebook asked Snopes and some other websites to band together as a coalition to verify any questionable stories published on the social platform. The coalition's responses would determine whether Facebook would allow the story in question to stay on the platform or whether it would be deprioritized by the Facebook algorithm.

It seemed a straightforward and worthy effort to the Snopes team who were already fact-checking news as a part of their normal course of business. However, not everybody saw it that way. As soon as Snopes began helping Facebook, it was viciously attacked as becoming a partisan, left-wing extremist website funded by George Soros, among others, and in Facebook's liberal pocket. By putting Snopes' credibility on the line, the criticism put its business at serious risk.

Snopes was calling out sites like America's Last Line of Defense (LLOD) which, at its height, was reportedly racking up more than one million clicks per month. LLOD billed itself as a political satire site and contested the fact-checking and deprioritizing done to its stories. However, most readers wouldn't notice the LLOD disclaimers which were not always easy to see. LLOD was doing too good a job of convincing people that its satire was indeed fact! LLOD wasn't just irritated that Facebook and Snopes were limiting its reach—there was something else going on too.[30]

Facebook shared that once an article was debunked by Facebook's fact-checking partners, its reach in the Facebook newsfeed dropped by up to 80 percent after an average of three days.[31] This decrease in traffic would make it incredibly difficult for LLOD to make any money. That's why LLOD went on the offensive and began criticizing and defaming Snopes, accusing it of being unable to differentiate between news and satire and burying satire stories when it shouldn't have. LLOD was desperate as the reduction in reach on Facebook meant that it wouldn't be able to attract advertisers as easily as it had done in the past. The harsh barrage of criticism hurt Snopes' reputation, created friction within its team, and even led to funding challenges.

In the end, Snopes was vindicated. When a third-party service fact-checked the company's analysis of media stories, it found them to be 100 percent accurate.[32] Research has also verified that all of Snopes' revenue comes from advertising, and the ad money does not affect its assessment of sources. The troubling upshot, though, is that in the post-trust era of fake news, even totally unbiased arbiters of truth are all too easily demonized.

Don't get us wrong: we think fact-checking is important and endorse it wholeheartedly. We're delighted that many media companies have embraced the practice. But we know that more is required. If we are to inoculate ourselves from manipulation and help in combating the epidemic, we have to understand the many ins and outs about how our mental biases lead us to fall prey to, and actually abet, fakery. Once we know about the machinations, we can coach ourselves to bear them in mind and rigorously consider which of them might be persuading us about any given claim we're finding compelling. This is critically important in the post-truth world of facts and alternative facts.

Fortunately psychologists have done a remarkable job of uncovering our biases. In the chapters that follow, we will further explore how they have been at play in many recent headline-making events, grouping them according to other human glitches that subconsciously drive us into these traps. When we understand those motivations, those deeply ingrained drives to believe falsehoods, we become highly motivated to counter them with the extraordinary counter-force of rational analysis to make our leaps of trust more judiciously.

GET SAVVY NOW
PROTECTING YOURSELF FROM ALTERNATIVE FACTS

- **Protect yourself:** One solution against falling for alternative facts is *inoculation.*
    - Inoculation is analogous to vaccinations in which people acquire immunity against a disease by being exposed to a weak form of it. Similarly, people can develop resistance against misinformation by being exposed to a small amount of it.
    - Research has found that the most effective way to inoculate someone was by using a two-pronged approach: (1) general inoculation—simply warning that the information may be misleading; and (2) specific inoculation—highlighting specific claims that are false. They provided evidence that through this process, people can be "vaccinated" against fake news.

- **Use reflection as a tactic to override bias:** Researchers have found that the ability to reflect is what predicts whether a person can distinguish facts from alternative facts. When forming an opinion, consciously choose to delay arriving at your judgment. Let all the available information sink in and deliberately reflect on it.

- **Resist repetition:** The first step in overriding bias due to repetition is recognizing that the bias exists and may be coloring your judgment. Don't get swept up by the momentum of alternative facts. Resist it.

- **Engage openly with dissent:** Actively engage with all parties involved in a particular disagreement. Try to get as much of a 360-degree view of the issue as you can before you form any judgments.

- **Challenge opinion and ask for facts:** For business leaders, force an evidence-driven approach to decision-making within your company. Ask for evidence when strong opinions are expressed. Vigorously challenge opinions that are not grounded in fact and don't give them equal treatment to those based on hard evidence.

CHAPTER 3

● ● ● ● ●

WE DESPERATELY WANT TO BELONG

"This is one of the most epic failures in corporate governance
in the annals of American capitalism. They did nothing to
verify that her scientific claims were true."
— JOHN CARREYROU, author of *Bad Blood: Secrets
and Lies in a Silicon Valley Startup*

LONELINESS KILLS

THERE IS NOTHING ESSENTIALLY WRONG WITH THE DESIRE TO BELONG.
It's important that we adhere to norms that establish what's right or wrong
in a given group—and belonging provides vital support and affirmation.
I am because we are. I am human because I belong. That is the crux of
the South African Ubuntu philosophy, which speaks to the intercon-
nectedness of the individual and community. Desmond Tutu describes

Ubuntu as the essence of being human.[1]

Belonging is a primal human need. Wanting to be a part of a group is what drives us to join sports clubs, go to parties, and establish connections with others. Countless studies have highlighted the mental and physical health benefits of simply belonging to a group. People with more social ties are happier, live longer, and have fewer ailments than their reclusive peers.

A recent Harvard study found that those with social ties outlived their isolated counterparts by an average of two and a half years.[2] The longitudinal study, begun in 1938, tracked 268 Harvard sophomores. (An interesting fact: while at Harvard, John F. Kennedy was recruited for this study). The control group was Boston inner-city residents. The astonishing finding of the study was that close relationships, *more* than money, notoriety, IQ, or even genes, delayed physical and mental health declines. That finding showed across all study participants—Harvard men and inner-city residents. Positive ties led to longer and happier lives. Robert Waldinger, director of the study, summed it up: "Loneliness kills."

A sense of belonging is generally a good thing. But we must be keenly aware of the subconscious ways in which our desire to be loyal to a group, and to be seen as loyal, can lead us to lose our integrity, common sense, and critical decision-making skills. There's nothing wrong in wanting to belong, but it is critical to do so for the right reasons.

A SILICON VALLEY HORROR SHOW

Can you imagine a company going from being one of the most innovative and groundbreaking biotechnology pioneers in the world with a market capitalization of $9 billion to an empty shell in a mere two years? What if you were an employee at that company, exhilarated by the prospect of working on something that was going to transform health care? What would it have felt like when it all started to crumble? Would you have seen it coming? Might you have been complicit in what we now know to have been one of the biggest frauds in the history of Silicon Valley?

Well, these are precisely the type of questions employees of Theranos pondered as the company went from being the golden child of corporate America, with its CEO Elizabeth Holmes gracing the covers of *Fortune*, *Forbes*, and *Inc.*, to a pariah, exposed by the *Wall Street Journal* as a scam and investigated by the Federal Drug Administration (FDA). What made the company's demise all the more painful was that many of the employees didn't know what was going on behind the scenes and were left in the lurch. Theranos, which claimed it had developed a new method of blood testing that would revolutionize medicine, had been a highly secretive operation, and most employees knew little about what those on other teams were working on.[3]

The company was no less secretive with investors and the scientific community. Under the guise of protecting trade secrets, Theranos published little data in peer-reviewed journals describing how its blood testing devices worked or attesting to the quality of its results.[4] Investors could only come onboard on the condition that they wouldn't ask questions about the underlying technology or company operations. Yet while the collapse may have seemed sudden and was startling even to insiders, the signals of looming disaster were flashing in plain sight for anyone to notice. Most paid no heed, instead trusting blindly—relishing in their being a part of the company.

At the heart of the Theranos "see no evil" story is one of the most powerful motivators of misplaced trust—our innate desire to *belong*. That drive leads us to fall prey to a number of biases that lead to poor judgments. Here we'll explore the cognitive traps our desire to belong leads us into and how we can be savvy about spotting the warning signs when we're at risk of being duped. There's no better place to start than by digging into the details of the Theranos debacle.

Headquartered in Palo Alto, California, Theranos set out in 2003 to reinvent blood testing. The aim was to develop devices that could conduct tests using microscopic amounts of blood and automate the process of analyzing it. The company eventually created a vessel for collecting blood samples that it called a "nanotainer" and an analysis machine it dubbed the "Edison." Typically, a blood test requires an injection with a long needle and the collection of several blood-filled vials, with the results taking several days to be reported. Holmes claimed to have invented a method for conducting and analyzing blood tests that was significantly faster and only required a drop or two of blood pricked from your finger. The drops were stored in the nanotainers and analyzed through the Edison machines. In addition to saving time and sparing patient discomfort, Holmes argued this would be a much cheaper method compared to the existing solutions from companies like Quest Diagnostics and the Laboratory Corporation of America. The innovation was hailed as a monumental scientific achievement.[5]

Growth came quickly to Theranos as it started making its testing available to several hospital systems in America. It partnered with Walgreens in 2013 and opened testing centers in forty-one Walgreens pharmacies with plans to open in thousands more. The company also began discussions with the Cleveland Clinic. Everything was going according to plan for Elizabeth Holmes who saw herself as the next Steve Jobs, even mimicking how he dressed. Investors, which included the likes of the Walton family ($150 million), Rupert Murdoch ($121 million), Betsy DeVos ($100 million), and the Cox family ($100 million), were all thrilled.[6] The board of directors, which was just as glamorous, included Riley Bechtel (former CEO of the Bechtel Group), Richard Kovacevich (former chairman and CEO of Wells Fargo), James Mattis (current Secretary of Defense), and Fabrizio Bonanni (former EVP of Amgen). With this star-studded cast, what could go wrong?[7]

In reality, a lot was going wrong, and had been wrong for a while. According to the *Washington Post*, in 2012 the FDA received a formal inquiry from the US Department of Defense to study the Theranos blood test devices.[8] That was even before the devices were commercially available. Later, as Business Insider found, the FDA's inspection reports from 2014 and 2015 stated unequivocally that the nanotainers were "not validated under actual or simulated use conditions" and "were not reviewed and not approved by designated individual(s) prior to issuance."[9] As a response to the FDA at the time, Theranos announced that it would voluntarily suspend most of its tests.

Matters went from bad to worse in October 2015 when the *Wall Street Journal* reported in an explosive piece of investigative journalism by John Carreyrou which claimed Theranos was using traditional blood-testing machines, such as those provided by Siemens AG, to run its tests as the company's own Edison machines were yielding inaccurate results. With former employees as sources, the article stated that its Edison machines could do just a fraction of all the tests that Theranos promised they were capable of—insinuating that Theranos was lying. Based on the story, Walgreens suspended its plans to expand blood-testing centers in their stores. The Cleveland Clinic announced that it would work to verify Theranos' technology further.[10]

By June 2016, Theranos was under investigation by federal prosecutors as well as the Securities and Exchange Commission (SEC) for allegedly misleading investors and government officials about its technology. At the same time, the US House of Representatives Committee on Energy and Commerce requested information regarding what Theranos was doing to correct its testing inaccuracies and adhere to federal guidelines. In April 2017, the same *Wall Street Journal* reporter said that an investor alleged Theranos had misled company directors about its technology and how it conducted the laboratory testing.[11] The lawsuit claimed Theranos had used a shell company to buy lab equipment to run fake demonstrations with secrecy. Carreyrou, the reporter behind the story, would later describe Holmes saying, "She is a pathological liar. She wanted to be a celebrated tech entrepreneur. She wanted to be rich and famous. And she wouldn't let anything get in the way of that."[12]

Theranos never recovered from the various allegations, investigations, and revelations. It was shut down in the summer of 2018. Nearly a billion dollars that was invested evaporated and hundreds of hard-working employees who had given up lucrative Silicon Valley jobs to join Theranos were left with absolutely nothing. It was the embodiment of fakeness and misplaced trust in the corporate world. All because of a pathological liar. Or was there more to the story?

We'd like to believe that Theranos is the exception to the rule, and that most companies in corporate America are run professionally with disciplined leaders, ethical business practices, mature cultures, responsible employees, and fact-based, transparent information sharing. However, while Theranos may be an extreme case, it is by no means the only example of a problem that goes well beyond having a flawed leader. Often employees know when there's a serious issue within a company but fail to do anything about it. A recent *Leadership IQ* survey captured what we are referring to—59 percent of employees are concerned about "fake news" and 64 percent are concerned about "alternative facts" within their companies.[13] When delving deeper into the survey, one also finds that individual contributors (65 percent) are more worried about fakeness than either middle managers (55 percent) or executives (53 percent). When people are so worried, why don't they share what they know more widely? Some of the employees at Theranos knew about the pathological lying. Why didn't any of them do something sooner? What did the board know and when?

When companies engage in fraud or mislead investors and consumers, the deception is rarely, if ever, perpetrated by a single leader acting in isolation. The deception is aided and abetted by a cast of players. Why? Part of the answer is the basic human desire to belong to a group. While that desire can be the positive force driving appreciation of others, altruism, and cooperation, it can also lead to collusion, willful blindness and skewed perception. Psychological research has produced some shocking examples of just how willing most people are to go along in order to get along, and how their perceptions are actually subconsciously warped in favor of group interests.

TWO FOOTBALL GAMES IN ONE

Dartmouth and Princeton squared off in their last game of the season at Palmer Stadium, Princeton, New Jersey on November 23, 1951. Princeton had won every single game of the season up to that point. Their all-American quarterback, Dick Kazmaier, was graduating that year.[14] He had been featured on the cover of *Time* magazine, and would go on to become the last Ivy League player to receive the Heisman Trophy. In the spring of 1952, he was selected by the Chicago Bears in the NFL draft, but decided to attend Harvard Business School instead.

Much was at stake for both teams. The Dartmouth Indians wanted to exact revenge, as they had lost to Princeton the preceding year. The Princeton Tigers, on the other hand, wanted a proper send off for their beloved quarterback. A few minutes into the game, it became obvious that both teams were playing to win at all costs. Play was very rough, with many penalties issued to both sides. Princeton fans went berserk when Kazmaier was forced to leave the game in the second quarter with a broken nose and a mild concussion. Matters went from bad to worse when in the third quarter, the Dartmouth quarterback sustained a broken leg while being tackled in the backfield. After the dust settled, Princeton had won with a final score of 13-0.

While the game itself was a mesmerizing battle, it is often remembered for a very different reason. In reading about the game in the respective college newspapers, psychologists Albert Hastorf of Dartmouth and Hadley Cantril of Princeton observed that the newspapers published two very divergent accounts of the game. It was as if each publication was reporting on two completely different games. This was particularly interesting to the two psychologists since each had studied at one school and then taught at the other. Hadley Cantril had studied at Dartmouth before moving to Princeton while for Albert Hastorf it was the opposite.

A week after the game, Hastorf and Cantril recruited students to review its video footage and answer questions about what they saw. By this time, a furor of editorials about the game had appeared in the campus papers at both schools. Though they'd watched the *exact* same footage, students from each school perceived the game very differently. Fans from Princeton reported seeing nearly twice as many rule infractions committed by the Dartmouth Indians as did the Dartmouth fans. Dartmouth fans believed Princeton players were primarily responsible for the rough game.

One specific question was, "Which team do you feel started the rough play?" While, a whopping 86 percent of the Princeton students said that Dartmouth had, only 36 percent of the Dartmouth students said their school was the culprit. When asked, "Do you believe the game was clean and fairly played or that it was unnecessarily rough and dirty?" 42 percent of the Dartmouth students said it was rough and dirty, while 93 percent of the Princeton students checked that box. A few years later, Hastorf and Cantril published a pioneering paper, "They Saw a Game:

A Case Study," introducing the concept of selective perception.[15] They reported that "out of all the occurrences going on in the environment, a person selects those that have some significance for him from his own egocentric position in the total matrix." The game "was actually many different games and that each version of the events that transpired was just as 'real' to a particular person as other versions were to other people." As this story illustrates, our perceptions are swayed by our motives: we tend to see what we want to see. And one of those distorting motives is to be seen as an upstanding member of a group. The Princeton students subconsciously wanted to believe that Dartmouth was to blame, and that is indeed what they saw. Dartmouth fans wanted to believe that Princeton was to blame, and that is what they saw.

The Hastorf and Cantril findings help to explain why partisan dissension has become such a problem in the US. Certain pockets of the American population only watch Fox News dismissing news from broadcast outlets like CNN and MSNBC as fake news, and vice versa. Like those students watching the football game, they also suffer from selective perception. So strong is their partisan fealty that they distrust the reporting of the "other side" even if it's based on solid facts. Similarly, in the United Kingdom, newspapers have become increasingly partisan over the last few decades, with readers rarely shifting their loyalties away from their favorite newspapers because over time, others don't seem factual anymore. They read newspapers that agree with their worldview and often genuinely don't understand the opposing viewpoint. The problem has become so extreme in regard to politics that it has itself become news, and even still, blatantly partisan reporting is wildly popular.

Let's take another more recent example of selective perception. The United Kingdom voted to exit the European Union (EU) on June 23rd, 2016. Colloquially known as the Brexit vote, many in the country were surprised by the results and couldn't believe that a majority of their fellow citizens had voted the way they did. The shock was felt the greatest in London, the capital of the United Kingdom and the most global city in the country. The Londoners had been in favor of staying in the European Union by a margin of 60 to 40. They assumed that the rest of the country would share their opinion. The polls also showed the country staying in the European Union. When the results were announced, the majority of the country had voted against staying in the European Union. The margin outside of London was significant enough to sway the entire vote. The Londoners shouldn't have been so shocked, but they were. They were so focused on the economic benefits to staying in the EU that they didn't read the rest of the country's mood for who the perceived sovereignty and immigration benefits of existing were much more important. It was a fatal case of selective perception.

Selective perception not only clouds our view of events and assessments of people and information, it sometimes causes us to overlook even outright falsehoods and wrongdoing perpetrated by the group we want to belong to. The degree of our willingness (subconscious as it may be) to throw our support behind egregious falsehood was demonstrated in one of the most famous of all psychology experiments.

HOW LONG IS THAT LINE?

In 1950, Solomon Asch, Polish psychologist and pioneer in social psychology, wanted to understand the nature of social conformity to answer two critical questions: (1) To what extent do social forces alter people's opinions and (2) Which aspects of group influence are the most important—the size of the majority or the unanimity of opinion? He conducted a fascinating study to seek the answers.[16]

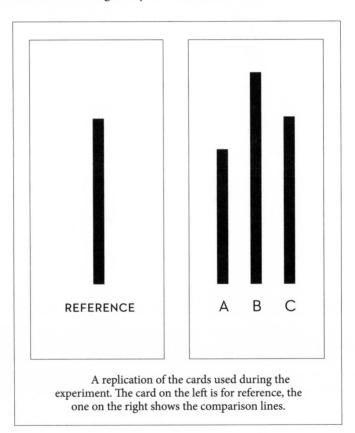

A replication of the cards used during the experiment. The card on the left is for reference, the one on the right shows the comparison lines.

Imagine walking into a room and being asked to sit at a table with seven other people. You are told that all of you are about to take part in a study about how people perceive things. Sounds simple enough. Unbeknownst to you, *all* of the other participants are actors. The experimenter arrives and places two cards in front of the group. The card on the left displays one vertical line, and the one on the right shows three vertical lines of varying length, one of which is the same length as the line on the left card. The experimenter asks each of you to choose which of the three lines on the right is the same length as the one on the left. You're then shown eighteen more sets of cards with lines of various lengths. As a control, the same set of cards is shown to someone who is alone in the room.

In the room with the group, the actors chose the correct line on the right-side card on six of the eighteen occasions. On the other twelve occasions, referred to as the "critical trials," however, they unanimously chose the wrong line. It seems obvious to you that they all are wrong, but how do you respond? Asch found that, on average, one-third of the participants went along with the majority view—even though it was clearly the wrong answer. Over the twelve critical trials, about three-quarters of the participants conformed at least once, while one-quarter of the participants never conformed. By comparison, in the control condition, with no pressure to conform, less than 1 percent of the participants gave the wrong answer. Group size played a strong role in whether subjects conformed: the bigger the group, the more likely the person was to conform. With one actor in the room, conformity was only 3 percent. With two actors, conformity increased to 13 percent, and with three or more actors, conformity increased to 32 percent. People actually felt pressure to overlook the truth about a mere line on a card. Imagine how much more powerful the pressure is when it's about something of actual consequence.

But you don't have to imagine, actually. You have almost surely experienced that pressure yourself. Have you ever been in a team meeting and had solid information on a matter but held back from sharing it because the majority of the people in the room thought otherwise? Or what about the scenario where you're new to a company and sitting in one of your first meetings with your new boss. She says something that's completely false but your peers around the table nod their heads in agreement. What do you do? Point out the mistake or go with the majority opinion? How about the scenario where the CEO of a company is about to make a major strategic decision and asks each of his direct reports for feedback? You're one of them and you know two things: first, that the decision your CEO is going to make is a bad one and second, that he's already made up his mind about moving forward regardless of what anyone in the room may say. In that scenario, do you speak up or bite your tongue and let it pass?

Sadly, we're all conditioned to bite our tongue. Sure, the truth is generally not as straightforward or obvious as the length of different lines on a card. But it is usually more obvious than we'd like to admit. Often, we are in possession of good information that we do not share with the group because we yearn to belong and so bend our beliefs to align with theirs. Not only is it human nature *not* to question an established majority, but we're taught from the time we're toddlers to be agreeable. Follow instructions, don't question the information that you're given, listen to your teacher, do what you're told, and behave just like the other kids in the class. As you become an adult, this translates to: follow your leader, abide by the unspoken rules of the company you work for, and don't question the information that's drip fed to you. Part of coming of age for most of us is learning to conform, which we're basically happy to do because life is much easier and more comfortable for us when we do.

Let's circle back to Theranos for a moment. Many of the company's employees were guilty of conformity. Some did not agree with the scientific integrity of the research or the management at Theranos, yet few said anything until *after* the company was questioned for fraud. On Glassdoor, an anonymous work review website, one employee described Theranos as follows: "No scientific integrity, not data driven (going into experiments with a wanted outcome and ignoring any data that shows otherwise), being put on projects that are clearly only PR driven, no attention to obvious glaring issues with the technology, upper management taking shortcuts...." That entry was dated September 2016, well after the *Wall Street Journal* exposed the fraud. Another employee stated in August of 2016 that he had joined Theranos "with the hopes and dreams that you were really part of something bigger. Possibly changing healthcare. Only to find out it was a big scam. Nothing worked. It was all of bunch of over hyped lies and deceptions."[17]

For the most part, employees played along with the narrative that Theranos was transforming healthcare. In part, this was because some of the employees were threatened by their managers with dire consequences if they didn't stay silent, as was revealed in the reporting after the company's collapse. But many, like the participants in the Asch study, chose the wrong stick in order to conform.

Even after all of the revelations from the investigations came out, some employees and investors still maintained their allegiance to Theranos. In March of 2018, some employees created a Space-Invaders-style video game in which players shot at photos of *Wall Street Journal* reporter, John Carreyrou.[18] The gun was the miniLab, the bullets were nanotainers, and the invader being shot at was Carreyrou. Tim Draper, billionaire investor and early backer of Theranos, said in a 2018 CNBC interview that Elizabeth Holmes was "bullied into submission" despite having done a "great job."[19] He was unable to come to terms with the deceit even when it was obvious that he and the other investors had made terrible mistakes. Solomon Asch concluded after his famous studies, "We have found a tendency to conformity in our society so strong that reasonably intelligent and well-meaning people are willing to call white black."[20] Too many employees and investors saw the black of misdoings at Theranos as white. Some felt that they had no choice, but many did.

Another of the most famous discoveries in psychology contributes additional insight into why the company could perpetrate its fraud so successfully. The company board was caught up in groupthink. This nefarious bias was illuminated by a study that examined what went wrong with the infamous Bay of Pigs disaster.

JOHN F. KENNEDY'S NIGHTMARE

"Let me tell you something. I have had two full days of hell—I haven't slept—this has been the most excruciating period of my life," President Kennedy told his confidant Clark Clifford in April 1961.[21] A few days earlier, Cuban guerrillas backed by the United States had invaded Cuba at the Bay of Pigs in the hopes of ousting Fidel Castro, the Cuban communist leader. Kennedy had wanted to overthrow Castro, and when the invasion plan (already in the works prior to him taking office), was introduced to him, he quickly approved it. The plan involved training Cuban exiles for an invasion of their homeland. A military operation involving two airstrikes against Cuban air bases would be carried out. Kennedy's advisors anticipated that the Cuban people, and even parts of the Cuban military, would support the invasion and Kennedy hoped it would give the US the upper hand in the Cold War.

Accounts from that period suggest that Kennedy quickly endorsed the plan because it fit his foreign policy ideology which was founded on the belief that democracies like the United States needed to have strong militaries and were required to demonstrate toughness against dictatorships around the world. Many argue that his analysis of the British appeasement of Nazi Germany while a student at Harvard influenced his thinking. Kennedy was also worried that Castro might trigger a series of revolutions across Latin America enabling that continent to spin out of the US's sphere of influence. During the preceding US elections, Kennedy had taken a firm stand on Cuba, promising to take action to overthrow Castro if he were elected. Some historians have emphasized that he felt obliged to keep those promises, but we know now there was more to it than that.

A few tactical elements explain why the invasion failed so horribly. First, when Kennedy approved the attack, he did so on the explicit condition that the US role in it be kept secret. As a result, the plans were adjusted and the invasion took place at the Bay of Pigs, 90 miles south of Havana and less conspicuous. The location posed a challenge—it was far from the mountains and, if the invasion failed, the guerrillas wouldn't have anywhere to fall back and hide. Second, once the operation was launched on April 15, 1961, B-26 bombers were supposed to destroy Cuba's air force. But they failed in that mission, missing many of their targets and leaving most of Castro's air force intact. Third, when the Cuban exile force approached the Bay of Pigs, coral reefs damaged their boats.[22]

Upon learning of the invasion, Castro acted swiftly and defiantly, immediately dispatching an overwhelming force to stave off the attack. He ordered roughly 20,000 troops to advance toward the beach and rounded up 100,000 civilian dissenters, squelching any potential momentum for a popular rising. To make matters worse for the rebels, Kennedy canceled the second air mission during the invasion because he got increasingly worried that the role of the US would be exposed. That enabled the Cuban air force to not only survive, but to attack the exile forces who were sitting ducks. The invasion strengthened the Castro regime and left the US embarrassed on the world stage.

Even assuming that the invasion was the right strategic decision, it doesn't explain why the execution plan was so flawed. The explanation is best captured in Kennedy's own words, "I must have been out of my goddamn mind to listen to those people. How could I have been so far off base? All my life I've known better than to depend on experts. How could I have been so stupid to let them go ahead?" Why did these experts have such a commanding influence over the President and how did they all get the invasion so wrong?[23]

The answers come from Yale psychologist Irving Janis who introduced the concept of groupthink in a landmark study in 1972. Using the Bay of Pigs and Kennedy's decision-making as one of two primary examples (the other being the Pearl Harbor attack in 1940), Janis studied the various events leading up to the invasion and showed the role groupthink played.[24]

It is easy to say that Kennedy should have questioned the soundness of the execution plan, but hindsight is always 20/20. However, there were indeed dissenters within his circle of advisors who did not believe the plan would succeed. Some even tried cautioning Kennedy but were ultimately unable to influence him. For the most part, Kennedy's advisors and Kennedy himself "uncritically accepted" the plan when it was first introduced to them. A few of his advisors such as Arthur M. Schlesinger Jr. and Senator J. William Fulbright had objections but minimized their doubts, self-censoring their views to maintain the group consensus. Schlesinger, for instance, presented his objections in a memo to Kennedy but suppressed his misgivings in team meetings. Attorney General Robert Kennedy privately admonished Schlesinger to support the invasion plan and in a team meeting, JFK called on each advisor *except* Schlesinger to vote for or against the plan. The fundamental problem was that the advisors had begun to so value being a part of the esteemed group that groupthink had taken hold of them.

In studying the Bay of Pigs fiasco and what happened at Pearl Harbor in December 1940, Irving Janis outlined three reasons groupthink clouds good judgment: (1) Pressure toward uniformity; (2) Overestimations of power and morality; and (3) Narrow-mindedness. To preserve and protect the tribe, group members suppress personal doubts, silence dissenters, and follow the group leader's suggestions. The group has excessive optimism in its mission and ability to execute on it. They believe in their members' inherent morality while stereotyping opposition as spiteful, biased, or foolish.

With the Bay of Pigs fiasco, the group of deciders was a new team that had just entered the White House. While each advisor wanted to prove his worth, they also wanted to be seen as collaborating well with the rest of the team. The advisors were also eager to please Kennedy, whose predisposition to crack down on the Cuban government was clear from his campaign. The group was also flush with a new sense of power and strongly believed in the moral superiority of the fight against communism. Additionally, JFK clearly signaled that dissent wasn't welcome by passing over Schlesinger in the discussion. Schlesinger expressed the bewitching effect of the groupthink that took hold years later writing "In the months after the Bay of Pigs I bitterly reproached myself for having kept so silent during those crucial discussions in the cabinet room. I can only explain my failure to do more than raise a few timid questions by reporting that one's impulse to blow the whistle on this nonsense was simply undone by the circumstances of the discussion."

Now take a step back and think about your own professional or personal circumstances. Reflect on situations in which you've prioritized the cohesiveness of the group so as not to ruffle feathers. Was the group overestimating its ability to achieve a goal? Did it have a sense of moral superiority about its commitment to the goal? Was anyone censored or brushed aside for expressing doubts about its merits? Have there been occasions where your manager has insisted that you and your peers collaborate to the point where you choose the cohesiveness of the group as more important than getting to the best answer? This is a more common occurrence in the business world than any of us would like to admit.

If you pick up the newspaper on any given day, you can comb through the sections and find plentiful instances of groupthink at work: in international affairs, domestic politics, business, and even in the arts and sports. Other high-profile cases of the perils of groupthink include the Salem witch trials, the space shuttle *Challenger* disaster, and the financial crisis of 2008. That fundamental desire of wanting to belong, be a part of something greater than oneself, and suspend critical thinking created groupthink and the errors in decision-making in each of these cases.

Returning to Theranos, we can see how groupthink biased the judgment of the board. The directors were revered leaders with decades of hardened experience from all walks of life. While they were not from the biotech industry, they knew a good deal about the proper management of companies and protecting the interests of investors. But the nature of the board membership contributed to groupthink which undermined the ability of all of the members to rigorously assess the company's operations.

Theranos first board member was Channing Robertson, a distinguished professor at Stanford University and Holmes original thesis advisor. He saw in Holmes a person who could be one of the most transformative entrepreneurs of the time. "When I finally connected with what Elizabeth fundamentally is, I realized that I could have just as well been looking into the eyes of a Steve Jobs or a Bill Gates," Robertson told *Fortune* magazine in 2014.[25] When Holmes came to Robertson informing him that she was going to drop out of Stanford, start a company, and revolutionize healthcare, asking him to join her in that mission, he eagerly agreed and jumped in as the first board member. He later became even more directly involved as an employee. Robertson believed that with the brilliance he had seen Holmes exhibit in the classroom and her charm with investors, she had the ability to transform an entire sector of the economy. He had a wildly inflated sense of her power.

The next board member to join was former Secretary of State George Shultz, who was captivated by Holmes' sense of purpose and, as he described it, her "purity of motivation." In all likelihood, he assumed that Robertson's early endorsement meant that the technical vision was sound too. A ten-minute initial conversation with Holmes turned into a two-hour meeting and within a month he joined the board. Here is where things get really interesting. Schultz went on to recruit practically every other board member which, in addition to James Mattis, Richard Kovacevich, and Riley Bechtel, included William Perry (former Secretary of Defense), Henry Kissinger (former Secretary of State), Sam Nunn (former US Senator), Bill Frist (former US Senator and heart-transplant surgeon), and Gary Roughead (Admiral, USN, retired).[26]

These distinguished individuals joined the board based on Shultz's recommendation without exercising their own due diligence. This set a precedent for how they would behave at every critical point in Theranos' history. The foremost job of any board director is to ask thoughtful questions and to test and verify the management team's decision-making logic on an ongoing basis. The board of Theranos consistently failed to do so.

When they should have been stress testing the business' operating practices, questioning assumptions independently, and seeking more information, the board of Theranos instead exclusively looked for data points that corroborated their vision for the company. Critical thinking and debates among board members were rare. Worse still, they operated with little information on which to make decisions. The board consistently interpreted ambiguous signals as supporting their existing hypotheses. It would appear that it was more important to them to belong to that esteemed group of directors than it was for them to independently perform the job they were hired to do. As a result, they presided over one of the most egregious business frauds on record.

US VERSUS THEM

The desire to belong to a group is also the culprit behind what's called ingroup bias. The term refers to people's tendency to favor members of their group over members of other groups: to think more highly of them, ascribe greater morality to them, and assess them as smarter and more trustworthy. In short, to see them as "better." This translates into an "us versus them" mentality, which is toxic, often leading to the demonization of the "other" and contributing to discrimination and sometimes violence. Both political and business leaders often build a following and amass power by stoking "us versus them" dynamics.

While this might be beneficial in a competitive context between companies, and in some cases even among teams competing for limited resources, it can quickly turn negative, leading to excessive loyalty and attacks on "others." A classic study known as Sherif's Robbers Cave experiment illuminated the conditions that fuel ingroup bias and the dynamics by which it operates. Muzafer Sherif, a Turkish American psychologist and his psychologist wife Carolyn Wood Sherif ran this experiment back in 1954.[27] Here's how it went.

Twenty-two twelve-year-old boys from similar backgrounds in Oklahoma were randomly divided into two groups. The boys were all from white, middle-class, two-parent Protestant backgrounds. The idea was to start with boys who were all as similar as possible to one another. None of the boys knew each other before the start of the study. The two groups were picked up by bus on successive days and transported to a 200-acre Boy Scouts of America camp at Robbers Cave State Park in Oklahoma. Upon arrival, the boys in each camp, unaware of the existence of the other group, were encouraged to bond with each other. Through various activities such as swimming and hiking, the boys developed an allegiance to their group, choosing group names like the Eagles and the Rattlers, and stenciling them onto shirts and flags.

In the second phase of the study, each camp was told about the other and pitted against one another in various competitions for limited resources—the Eagles versus the Rattlers. A series of fairly innocuous activities including tug-of-war and baseball were arranged, and the boys were informed that a trophy would be awarded to the group with the highest team score. The losing team would get no consolation prize. Each team was confident of winning and in conversations among themselves, overplayed their strengths while discounting the merits of the opposing team. The teams were also set up to benefit at the expense of the other. In one example, the winning team was allowed to go to a picnic site first and ended up finishing the food before the other team arrived.

Intergroup conflict was high, and the boys often exhibited hostile and even malicious behavior toward members of the opposing group.

At first, the two groups only verbally abused each other as animosity developed between them. However, verbal abuse soon turned into each group destroying the other's flags, ransacking one another's cabins and stealing private property. Before you knew it, both groups of boys became so aggressive that the researchers were forced to physically separate them. A two-day cooling off period was instituted, but even during this period, tensions ran high and the animosity remained. Each group described themselves in favorable terms while unequivocally disparaging the other group. Powerful ingroup biases had set in for these two groups of boys. These weren't street gangs but rather well-adjusted boys who, in a specific environment, exhibited behaviors that their parents wouldn't recognize in them.

The Sherifs concluded that when groups compete for limited resources as teams in a company oft do, they invariably come into conflict and ingroup members form negative attitudes toward the outgroup. Moreover, they saw that simple contact with the outside group alone wasn't enough to reduce the negativity. Other, more substantial measures needed to be taken such as forcing unity and cooperation to achieve common goals.

Near the end of the study, Sherif had engineered a situation in which the camp water supply had been cut off. The idea was that with a shared goal of restoring the supply (as Deutsch highlighted the importance of), the boys would work together. They would first have to locate the water tank on the top of the mountain, and then work together to remove rocks that Sherif and his research associate had placed over the valve.

Lo and behold, the boys quickly put aside their animosity. The boundaries between "us" and "them" faded and they worked well together to achieve a common goal.

The Sherif study shows just how easily our ingroup bias can be manipulated, and unfortunately politicians, and companies too, have learned that doing so can serve their interests. It is another way in which our desire to belong can be taken advantage of. Media companies, for one, have had a field day with fostering us versus them thinking. It is no secret that many journalists increasingly see their role as defending the points of views of their company's owners and the political leanings of their viewers and readers. Whether it is Fox News, CNN or MSNBC, the *New York Times*, *Wall Street Journal*, the *Guardian* (Manchester), the *Independent* (London) or the *Times* (London), an us versus them mindset is intentionally nurtured both within the organization and among its audience.

Does triggering ingroup bias engender loyalty among audiences? Most definitely. Does it hurt political discourse? Absolutely. It also leads to false divisions that can undermine social cooperation, with groups more intent on proving the "other" despicable than on solving pressing problems.

The bizarre extremes to which people are easily whipped up can be shown in stark relief by looking at a case in which group loyalty was based on preference for one of two kinds of sugared water.

THE COLA WARS

The "cola wars" was the name given to the marketing battles that Coca-Cola and PepsiCo fought over the course of three decades to win the hearts and minds of consumers. Through a series of innovative marketing strategies, advertising campaigns, promotions, and product extensions, each company constantly tried to outdo the other and win greater market share. Pepsi, as the challenger brand with the smaller market, often took the lead as disrupter, upending the status quo and catching its competitor off balance. Coca-Cola would respond furiously, fighting to retain the consumers Pepsi was gunning for. The competition became even more fierce when sales stopped growing as consumers moved away from carbonated beverages to healthier drinks.

Consumers avidly took sides in the competition. You were either a Coke drinker or Pepsi drinker, and people rarely drank both or switched sides. Loyalists watched the Super Bowl ads of their brand with glee and disparaged those of the competitor. Researchers of a 2016 study analyzed a database on consumer shopping history for more than sixty-two thousand households across the US. Results showed that consumers were remarkably loyal to their chosen brand. Coca-Cola kept 94 percent of its loyal households from one quarter to the next and Pepsi retained 91 percent of its households.[28]

Inside the companies, loyalty and the competitive spirit were intense. Having worked for PepsiCo, one of the co-authors has firsthand knowledge of how the cola wars affected the company. As an employee, you never ever drank Coca-Cola products. We all knew that to be caught with a Coke in our hand was company betrayal. But that hardly mattered, as few, if any, employees *wanted* to drink a Coke. The cola wars were personal. We took the competition very seriously—the mere sight of a Coca-Cola was an irritant. Business partners were strongly encouraged to only serve Pepsi at meetings and to hide all Coca-Cola products. PepsiCo leaders were known to leave social events in a huff if Coca-Cola products were being served. One year, at the annual sales meeting, a PepsiCo manager even distributed floor mats depicting a crushed coke can with the message, "wipe your feet here" on it to the thousands of attendees attending as a way to motivate the sales teams to *crush* the competition. Employees knew that if they were to leave PepsiCo and join the Coca-Cola Company they'd be seen as making peace with the devil! No one ever did that. And in case you were wondering, all of this was true for Coke too. In 2013, a Coke driver was fired for drinking a Pepsi in the back room of a California store after completing a delivery.[29] He'd been with Coca-Cola for twelve years.

Yet, as in the Robber's Cave experiment, when the companies were given an opportunity to collaborate for a greater good, they became effective partners. In 2012 they joined forces against Mayor Bloomberg's health campaign linking consumption of sodas to obesity in New York City.[30] Bloomberg proposed a Soda Ban which would limit the sale of soft drinks over sixteen ounces. Coca-Cola and Pepsi launched a PR assault against the ban, and both together and individually lobbied against health bills designed to reduce consumption of their products. They wanted to educate consumers about obesity in a more balanced fashion, emphasizing what they were doing to help. Then, in 2015, they came together again to help veterans get jobs, jointly running public service announcements encouraging companies to hire veterans.[31] In those ads, each company's CEO raised a toast to veterans (with their favorite cola in their hands). As we've seen, the two companies can certainly partner, but why would they? Both have masterfully engineered bias to their benefit. For employees and consumers, being loyal to one group over the other satisfies the fundamental human motivation to belong.

GET SAVVY NOW
HOW TO FIGHT THE NEED TO BELONG

- **Encourage those who don't conform:** Studies have found that non-conforming employees report being more confident and engaged in their work, display greater creativity, and receive higher ratings on performance and innovativeness from their supervisors. Make space in your company for non-conformity.

- **Why some people don't conform:** About ¼ of subjects in Asch's study never agreed with the erroneous judgment of the majority. Those that resisted said (1) they were confident of their own judgment and (2) they felt like they had to be true to their own perceptions.

- **Fight against groupthink:** In combating conformity and groupthink, managers should (1) emphasize the need for all viewpoints, including dissenting ones; and (2) build a culture that encourages critical thinking and transparency. When you hire, look for heterogeneous employees.

- **Hold off on voicing your own opinions:** Being a manager means that you shouldn't be the first to speak. Try to create an environment where your teams develop their opinions first and then come to you for validation.

- **Devil's advocate:** Always assign one person to play the devil's advocate when trying to solve a problem. Discuss the final idea with outsiders to get impartial opinions.

- **Welcome competition:** Don't treat your competitors like they're enemies. It can lead to a culture of ingroup bias where you're not only disrespectful to your competitors, but also blind to their strengths and advantages. Competition is healthy; it makes us work harder and more creatively. However, even as we compete, we should find ways to partner around shared values.

CHAPTER 4

WE WANT TO BE RIGHT

"The four most beautiful words
in our common language: I told you so."
—GORE VIDAL

ONE SHORT LIFE

TRAYVON BENJAMIN MARTIN SHOULD NOT BE A HOUSEHOLD NAME. HE was an ordinary seventeen-year-old high school student from Miami Gardens, Florida. Trayvon enjoyed video games and football. He cut grass, babysat, and washed cars to earn his own money. Martin excelled in math, studied aeronautical engineering, and took after-school classes to further his interest in aviation. His teachers described him as respectful, well-mannered, and studious.

For his junior year, his mother shifted him to a much larger high school which she thought would be a better fit for him. Unfortunately, he didn't do as well in his new school and began to display behavioral issues. He was serving a ten-day suspension from school for carrying a marijuana pipe and an empty bag containing marijuana residue on one fateful day in February 2012.

At the time, Martin had gone with his father to visit Brandy Green, his father's fiancée, at Green's townhouse in the gated community of Retreat at Twin Lakes in Sanford, Florida. On the evening of February 26, 2012, he was walking back alone to Green's house after purchasing a bag of Skittles and an Arizona iced tea from a nearby convenience store. The neighborhood was not safe. It had suffered several burglaries, thefts, and one shooting that year. In the preceding twelve months, police were called to the Retreat 402 times. The previous fall the community had set up a neighborhood watch program, for which George Zimmerman was made coordinator. Zimmerman took his role very seriously and called the police often to report people whom he suspected of suspicious activities. Each time he called, Zimmerman offered information on the race of the suspect. All were black males, as was Trayvon Martin.

Zimmerman noticed Martin walking back from the convenience store while he was driving through the neighborhood on a personal errand. Having never seen Martin before, he was immediately suspicious. Martin fit the profile of one of his suspects from a few weeks earlier. He called the police dispatcher, telling him that he saw a suspect who seemed up to no good and that he was following him in his car. The dispatcher thanked Zimmerman for the information and asked him to stop following Martin. Zimmerman continued to do so. A short while later, Trayvon Martin lay dead on the ground with a bullet wound to his chest. He was seventy yards from Green's home. Zimmerman found himself standing over Martin explaining to the police that he had shot him in self-defense. There was no video and no witnesses who could corroborate Zimmerman's story.

Almost instantaneously, the case turned into a media frenzy. News outlets heavily covered the story in the ensuing weeks, and polarizing narratives quickly developed. The narratives depicted Martin as either a thug or an ordinary kid, while Zimmerman was depicted as either a right-wing-reactionary or an honest-and-concerned-citizen. People reflexively formed opinions based on their existing beliefs and fell into either the pro-Zimmerman or pro-Martin camp. Civil rights activists waded into the debate along with political pundits, politicians, and even President Obama, who said "If I had a son, he'd look like Trayvon."[1]

The public took predictable positions driven by their own personal life context and mental lenses. The truth was more complex than any of the prevailing narratives, but media accounts for the most part simplified it and chose sides, crafting their stories to please public preferences in the quest for readership and ratings. In the end, two tragedies took place, the first of which was Trayvon Martin's death. The second was the media's exploitation of the story.[2]

But the media only carried part of the blame. Some of it also rested with the bias of its audiences to see distorted views of the events. This was due to the cognitive glitch known as confirmation bias, the tendency to interpret all new information as confirming one's existing beliefs. We want to be right and we look for information that supports our existing beliefs.

Perhaps you've heard of confirmation bias before. After all, it was discovered decades ago and has been written about extensively since. Cognitive psychologist Peter Cathcart Wason discovered it in studies he conducted in the 1960s.[3] Wason found that people tend to seek out information that supports (rather than challenges) their existing beliefs, and to deem confirming information as more credible. That's exactly what happened in the case of Trayvon Martin. Even if they were watching or reading responsibly balanced coverage, pro-Martin people focused on the parts of the story that substantiated their worldview while the pro-Zimmerman camp did the same. This in turn fed the fires of fake news, which whipped across the internet, and the more audiences showed their appreciation of the fake news, the more its producers manufactured.

REFUSING TO BE WRONG

The news coverage of Trayvon Martin's death did not change people's opinions on where guilt lay for the events that transpired on February 26, 2012. That is because our minds are hardwired to privilege information that confirms our existing beliefs. Let's look at a seminal study of confirmation bias to better understand this phenomenon. In 1979, Charles Lord and his colleagues from Stanford University recruited students with strong and opposing views about capital punishment.[4] Half were in favor of it, judging the death penalty to be a good deterrent of crime; half were against it, asserting that an eye-for-eye did nothing to decrease crime. The students were presented with studies that either confirmed or denied the effectiveness of the death penalty. The studies were fictitious and presented equally compelling statistics for both sides of the argument.

The findings were striking. Evidence confirming the effectiveness of the death penalty strengthened people's views about capital punishment *if* they were initially in favor of it. Those people dismissed the studies against the death penalty, claiming the statistics were unconvincing.

The reverse was true for students who initially opposed the death penalty. They found the evidence against capital punishment as compelling, while dismissing the studies in favor of it. Those who started out in favor of capital punishment were now even more resolute in their beliefs, as were those who opposed it.

Even if you've known about confirmation bias, you are almost surely still falling into its trap regularly. Becoming aware of our cherry-picking of information that supports our views is quite difficult. That's in part because so many biased sources of information are available, which portray themselves as truthful. But it's also due to another bias that helps us close our minds to offending inputs. It's called the backfire effect.

OBAMA AND TESLA

Barack Obama is a Muslim. This mistruth first surfaced in 2004 as President Obama was campaigning for the US Senate. The lie hit the larger political stage in 2008 after his election as president and seemed to take on a life of its own. In 2010, a Pew Research poll showed that 31 percent of Republicans believed Obama was a Muslim. For many people who believed the claim, no amount of refutation could debunk it. The more air time the denial of this statement received, the more the coverage seemed to convince people that Obama was indeed of the Muslim faith. In 2015, a whopping 54 percent of Republicans believed Obama was a Muslim. They subconsciously wanted to be right so much that no amount of denial could change that. With every point of refutation, they dug their heels in deeper.[5]

The irony of the backfire effect is that corrections of falsehoods are not only ineffective, they serve to *increase* the dedication of believers to those falsehoods. Dartmouth College professor Brendan Nyhan and University of Exeter professor Jason Reifler demonstrated this in a series of experiments in which subjects were presented with fake newspaper articles that confirmed common misperceptions.[6] One such article reported there were weapons of mass destruction (WMDs) in Iraq. When subjects were given corrective articles explaining that WMDs were never found, liberals who opposed the war readily accepted the new information and rejected the old. Conservatives, on the other hand—who supported the war—did the opposite, and then some: they reported being even more convinced that there were WMDs. They went so far as to argue that Saddam Hussein must have hidden or destroyed them. Why do we behave this way? Nyhan and Reifler say it's because counter information "threatens our worldview or self-concept."

The backfire effect not only makes us impervious to information we don't like, it intensifies our loyalty if those we believe in are criticized. Consider the devotion of Tesla fans. The company is both one of the most innovative and controversial of our time, and the controversy has significantly benefited Tesla's bottom line.

Rarely does a week go by without there being an issue concerning Tesla in the news. From its capacity to self-drive, its ability to produce Model 3 sedans fast enough, or the pronouncements of its occasionally obnoxious but brilliant CEO, Elon Musk, Tesla has time and again found itself in hot water. In 2013, the New York Times described fundamental flaws in the battery life of the Model S sedan, claiming the range was severely compromised while driving in below-freezing temperatures.[7] Musk responded with a string of tweets, calling the article "fake." In 2017, Tesla owners filed a class action lawsuit, claiming that Tesla exaggerated the capabilities of its autopilot functionality.[8] The company responded, asserting the lawsuit was a "disingenuous attempt to secure attorney's fees." In 2018, the Center for Investigative Reporting published a piece concluding that Tesla under-reported worker injuries to make its safety record appear better than it was. The company called the investigation an "ideologically motivated attack by an extremist organization ... create a calculated disinformation campaign against Tesla."[9] To make a long story short, Tesla has accrued its fair share of critics among consumers, employees, journalists, industry watchers, and financial analysts.

Yet the steady drumbeat of criticism and refutations has driven Tesla fans deeper into their pro-Tesla echo chambers. Some have described Tesla fans as a "cult of zealots that are incapable of criticizing the company."[10] With each new negative news story, fans have grown more defiant, arguing more passionately about the merits of the company to anyone who would listen. Fans also continued to buy Tesla's cars in droves. All the coverage has been fantastically potent (free) advertising. For a company that was only producing a mere one hundred thousand cars a year (compared to General Motors which sold ten million vehicles during the same period), the controversies generated an outsized amount of attention. One result was that a record number of people signed up to join the waitlist for Tesla's Model 3 even before they had an opportunity to test-drive it or learn about its features. It is too early to tell whether those Tesla fans are misguided or not in their defense of the company, but we do know that in the summer of 2018, the Model 3 was the hottest-selling car in its category.

If you begin to look for the backfire effect, you will quickly see examples of it in all parts of your life — from your personal relationships, to companies you work for, and teams you work with. Think about situations in which you've been involved. Maybe you had an argument with someone about the allocation of tax relief in the bill signed by President Trump who simply refused to acknowledge the facts. Or maybe it was a disagreement with your boss, after which he doubled-down on a strategy you gave him strong evidence against. Perhaps it was a disagreement with your spouse about whether to send your child to public or private school—the more you made a case for one, the more your spouse became convinced of the other. Now reflect on situations in which you may have been the one digging in your heels.

The backfire effect is among the most insidious of psychological phenomena involved in the crisis of trust. So, what can you do to avoid triggering it? You need to be extremely mindful of how your arguments are perceived. If you have to explain over and over again what is blindingly obvious to you, and you've presented objective information as backup, and your interlocutor still won't budge, you have just strengthened the opposition to your cause. Don't assume that the reason they're not agreeing is that they don't understand. People typically understand an argument quickly; whether they'll ever agree is another matter entirely. You should consider taking a different tack.

It is essential to appeal to people not only through intellectual argument, but also by engaging their emotions. Arguments aren't just won on facts but also on feelings. When you're trying to make a case, whether to a friend, your team or boss, and you sense they're digging into their position, try to think of a way to appeal to their heart. It is easier to disagree with logic than it is with emotion. Rather than trying to beat them down with competing facts, soften them up by appealing to their basic human empathy.

Let's take a quick look at the power of appealing to people's hearts. Aylan Kurdi, a three-year-old Syrian boy, made global headlines after he drowned in the Mediterranean Sea.[11] The Syrian refugee crisis had been going on for over a year before the iconic image of his lifeless body on the beach shook the world. Until then, many people did not seem all that bothered by the humanitarian crisis. But Aylan's image tugged at people's heart-strings and spurred them into action. Record donations for refugee relief poured in. The same response followed the press coverage of a two-year-old girl named Yanela Sanchez, crying at the US Border Patrol checkpoint along the border with Mexico. The image spread like wildfire across international newspapers — she became the face of the immigration debate even though she wasn't one of the children who were separated from their parents. People rallied all around the country, fundraising to support changes to US immigration policies.[12]

Another powerful method of combating the backfire effect is to present information in a non-confrontational manner. Show that you understand the other person's point of view and find some point of common ground with their thinking. You will be much more effective in persuading them than if you attack them.

PLAYING THE BLAME GAME

Our intense desire to be right often leads us not only to cherry-pick information but to actually fabricate. Have you ever heard yourself make a claim to support your view and cringed inside because you knew that you'd just made up what you were saying, or put a disingenuous spin on it? Doing this is very common, even among usually honest people. It's especially common when we want to defend ourselves or others from being perceived as wrong. One of the most harmful ways we do this is by scapegoating, blaming others for our faults, or those of people in whom we've chosen to believe.

Had Yoko Ono not swooped in and stolen John Lennon's heart, the two wouldn't have gotten married, and John wouldn't have left the Beatles. The world would have continued to enjoy brilliant new music and performances from one of the most talented bands of all time. So goes this classic story of Yoko as a scapegoat.

Here's how the story began. Yoko met John in November 1966 at a gallery in London, where she was preparing an exhibition of her work. Her show was to open to the public the following day. The two instantly connected over Yoko's interactive art. In their first conversation, John asked to participate in her exhibition piece *Painting to Hammer a Nail* which invited visitors to hammer a nail into the canvas. Yoko flatly said no. She didn't know who the Beatles were (much less who John was) and didn't want to mess up her piece before it opened publicly. They eventually agreed: John would pay imaginary money to hammer in an imaginary nail. After the art show, the two—each of whom was married to someone else—continued their relationship. Months later, when John's wife Cynthia was away on vacation, Yoko and John collaborated on a sound collage and became lovers. Thus began their whirlwind romance. Roughly two and a half years later, they were married. Soon after, John announced his departure from the group and the Beatles broke up.

Did Yoko cause the band to break up or were they already on their way out? Beatles' fans around the world squarely blamed Yoko, but for anyone looking closely at the group's final years, it's clear that the members were going in different directions musically, romantically, and spiritually. They were also quite irritated with one another. By 1969, the "Fab Four" were barely speaking. Looking back, in 2012 lead singer Paul McCartney stated that Yoko "certainly didn't break the group up. I don't think you can blame her for anything. [John] was definitely going to leave [one way or another]."[13] But Beatles fans didn't want to see their heroes as the ones responsible for what they saw as a calamity.

The term scapegoating derives from ancient Israel and a ritual practiced on the Day of Atonement. Each year on this day two goats were summoned. The first goat was killed, and its blood sprinkled on the Ark of the Covenant. The High Priest would then lay his hands on the head of the second goat and confess the sins of the people. This goat had a luckier fate than the first: it was released into the wilderness—carrying with it the burden of the people's sins. Over time, this goat came to be known as the scapegoat.[14]

Scapegoating occurs for various reasons, but the most common is that we feel psychological relief when someone *else* is blamed when something goes wrong. When problems and disappointments arise, it's easier to point the finger, absolve ourselves of any role, and believe that the cause is "out there." This behavior often begins in childhood and stays with us through the course of our lives. Scapegoating is considered adaptive because of the psychological relief that it provides. It also, of course, causes a great deal of injustice. But calling people out on it can be quite tricky, as they'll often have staunch allies back them up. We saw this in the slowly emerging revelations of malfeasance by the upper management of Volkswagen, in the emissions scandal dubbed the "diesel dupe."[15]

In September 2015, the Environmental Protection Agency (EPA) found that many VW cars sold in the US contained software that could detect when they were being tested. The "defeat device" could sense test scenarios by monitoring speed, engine operation, air pressure, and even the bearings of the steering wheel. When a car was in controlled laboratory conditions (which generally involved putting them on treadmill-like machines called dynamometers) the device put the vehicle into a safety mode of sorts, in which the engine ran below its standard power and performance in order to lower emissions. When the car was back on actual roads, the device switched the engine out of this safety mode. The result was that the engines emitted over forty times the amount of nitrous oxide pollutants permitted by the EPA in the US when out on the country's roadways.

When the EPA discovered the fraud, Volkswagen's head of US business, Michael Horn, claimed the defeat device was the brainchild of rogue engineers. "This was a couple of software engineers who put this in for whatever reason. To my understanding, this was not a corporate decision. This was something individuals did."[16] This should have been immediately seen as subterfuge. Two lone rogue engineers wouldn't have had enough motivation to conduct such a huge fraud: the massive profits from it went to VW shareholders, not to them. Fortunately, fraud of such a scale is difficult to hide from senior management in most companies due to the various quality testing checks and balances that are in place. But if executive leaders are behind the fraud—or prefer not to admit it has been perpetrated— scapegoating can be quite effective in propping them up in their positions of power. That was true for a time with the VW case, but hard evidence was eventually turned up. A report was discovered that indicated that VW management had in fact received warnings in 2011 from VW technicians about the emissions practice.[17] The company failed to address the warnings and never gave a reason why. Ultimately, however, overwhelming evidence was compiled and the ex-CEO was charged with fraud.

In the VW case, the scapegoating was clearly and consciously perpetrated, but often when we scapegoat, we're not aware that we're doing it. Many Beatles fans really bought into Yoko Ono's blame. That's why whenever we find ourselves blaming someone or some group, we should take some time to seriously question whether we're being fair or may be casting our own guilt onto others, succumbing to our intense desire to be right.

BEING WELL-INFORMED IS NO MAGIC BULLET

So intense can our desire to be right be that it often leads us to project our own biases onto others. We are sure that they're the ones who are refusing to see the truth. This thinking error is called naive realism, defined as the tendency to believe that we see the world objectively and that those who disagree with us are uninformed, irrational, or biased. To see this perverse psychological mechanism in action, let's look at one of the most charged issues that has faced the world for decades: the Israeli-Palestinian conflict.

With a conflict that has been raging since Israel's founding in 1948, there's only one thing pro-Israeli and pro-Arab audiences agree on about media in the United States: it is extremely biased. The views of the two communities are diametrically opposed even when viewing the *exact same* material. The conflict has been viewed through a very thick lens of naive realism.

A number of laboratory investigations of naive realism have been conducted regarding news of the Israeli-Palestinian conflict. One of the first was done during the 1982 Lebanon War. Stanford psychologist Lee D. Ross and his research team showed 144 observers six different television segments about the war. The observers didn't just arrive at different conclusions, they saw two different worlds.[18]

In watching the video clips, pro-Arab viewers heard forty-two references painting Israel in a positive light, with twenty-six painting them negatively. In sharp contrast, pro-Israeli viewers watching the very same clips, spotted sixteen references that painted Israel positively and fifty-seven references that painted Israelis negatively! Furthermore, each group was adamant that they had counted correctly and saw the numbers as further proof that the media was biased, resulting in damaging views of the conflict. Depending on which side you aligned yourself with, you saw the event differently (selective perception). Naive realism was the bias involved in dismissing the opposing side as irrational and uninformed.

The study went on to find that bizarrely, participants who were most informed about the conflict were even more biased in their perceptions. That was because those participants felt the news stories lacked context. The more knowledgeable the participant, the more he or she felt important information was missing in the video clips that justified the behavior of their side and led to the bias in the broadcast coverage. Their side was not to blame, the biased media coverage was.

And here's the greatest irony of all: participants in the study were more likely to have polarized views about the video clips that were attempting to be balanced than they were about the news reports that were from obviously biased sources. According to the researchers, those drew fewer charges of bias.

This shows that watching out for bias in coverage is not as easy as simply choosing to rely on sources that are widely viewed as balanced. Not only may we elect to consider any given story that challenges our views as biased, but the reporters and experts sharing information are also not immune to the biases that allow us to be steadfast in thinking we are right. Lies and distortions aren't only spread from sources that are unabashedly biased. In fact, people who are held in high regard for their expertise, education, and experience may be propagating fake news with much greater success (intentionally or unintentionally) than anyone else.

Look at the world around you — who do you consider to be the most informed sources of information? As you absorb information from those people, keep in mind that they too may actually be biased because they could be suffering from a combination of confirmation bias, scapegoating, and naive realism—just like the rest of us. Also consider that the media sources you think of as being the most biased may actually be the most balanced of all. Hence the fake news conundrum: the sources you believe you should trust may be the most biased while the sources you criticize as being the most biased may actually not be!

SNAP DECISIONS

A final cognitive bias that abets us in believing that we are right is the overconfidence bias. Dubbed "the most significant of all the cognitive biases," it is the tendency to appraise ourselves as smarter and more capable than we are. The irony is that it can lead even very smart people to behave very stupidly.

"Sooo does anyone else not open Snapchat anymore? Or is it just me...ugh this is so sad."[19] With that one tweet by Kylie Jenner (to her 2.4 million Twitter followers) the stock dropped approximately 7 percent in a single afternoon. According to the YouGov BrandIndex, a daily online survey that tracks consumer opinion toward brands, user sentiment of Snapchat among its 18—34 demographic plunged 73 percent around the same time.[20] More than one million subscribers signed a petition demanding that Snapchat reverse direction and bring back its old design.

How could so much go wrong so quickly for a company whose market capitalization had also lost more than half its value in barely a year?

Source: Twitter.com retrieved on November 30th, 2018

To understand what happened, let's take a brief look at the history of Snapchat and its founder Evan Spiegel.[21] Born in 1990, Spiegel grew up in Santa Monica, California as the older son of two wealthy Ivy League lawyers. He was a student at an exclusive school in Santa Monica called Crossroads, which Tinder co-founder Sean Rad, Kate Hudson, Jonah Hill, Jack Black, and Gwyneth Paltrow all attended. His parents had a full-time housekeeper in their home, took their children holidaying to Europe each year and once even took Spiegel snowboarding via helicopter! When he turned eighteen, Spiegel asked his parents for a BMW 550i as a present to replace the Cadillac Escalade that he had been given when he received his driver's license at the age of sixteen. His father refused to buy him the car, so Spiegel moved in with his mother in protest. His parents had divorced by that point and his mother quickly leased him the $75,000 BMW.

After high school, Spiegel found his way to Stanford University (with his father's help in the form of charitable donations if reports are to be believed) where he studied product design. While there, Spiegel was a member of the Kappa Sigma Fraternity where, according to leaked emails from acquaintances, he was quite the partier. Because he was spending extravagantly, Spiegel was eventually given (and forced to adhere to) a monthly $2,000 allowance from his parents.

During that period, Spiegel signed up for some graduate classes and met Intuit co-founder Scott Cook who took a liking to him. Cook got Spiegel an internship working on a new product for the Indian market. That was an important connection as Cook ended up becoming an early investor in Snapchat which Spiegel founded while still at Stanford.

In 2011 a friend, Reggie Brown, lamented that there was no way to make the photographs he sent to his friends disappear. Evan Spiegel loved the idea and together with Bobby Murphy, the three of them started a company called Pictaboo.[22] It was renamed Snapchat later that summer when there was a disagreement over equity and Brown left. At that point, the app had all of 127 users. However, by 2012 high school students who were extremely conscious of the lack of privacy on the internet, started to take to Snapchat. Users suddenly swelled to 100,000 and continued to grow.

In the fall of 2012, Spiegel left Stanford a few credits shy of graduating to focus full time on the app. By this time, it was hitting a million users a day and growing even faster. In 2013, he rebuffed a $3 billion offer from Mark Zuckerberg of Facebook to acquire his company. Fast forward to the spring of 2017 — Snapchat launched an initial public offering on the New York Stock Exchange making him an instant billionaire. At this time, Snapchat had nearly 200 million daily active users and was considered the hottest social media company. Spiegel became the youngest public company CEO in America. He was hailed as a product genius of the ilk that few had seen since the likes of Steve Jobs.[23] His purity of vision, steadfastness and innate ability to understand millennials was lauded by the media. At a time when Facebook was seeing curbed usage on its platform and Twitter was trying to turnaround its flagging user numbers, Snapchat appeared to be on a very sharp growth trajectory.

But in reality, trouble was brewing beneath the surface. An event was halting its meteoric rise - Facebook's decision to copy Snapchat's most iconic feature, stories (disappearing posts) for its Instagram platform which, by this time, Facebook had purchased. That began the halting of growth on the Snapchat platform. To counter this, Spiegel launched a massive app redesign, which eventually led to the Kylie Jenner tweet. Users hated it. In August 2018, Snapchat reported that daily users had fallen from 191 million users in the first quarter to 181 million in the second.[24] Instagram Stories had more than 400 million daily users during the same period. For a social media platform that had been growing exponentially this was a sudden and humbling slowdown. This isn't a story about a failed redesign though. There was something more to it. Here's the backstory.

In 2016, Instagram Stories launched because Kevin Systrom, Mark Zuckerberg, and the rest of the team at Facebook saw Snapchat as a serious threat to their business. They believed the best way to minimize the threat was by copying its most impressive feature. Afterall, imitation is the sincerest form of flattery. What was Spiegel's response to the

Facebook salvo? According to a *Businessweek* story from the summer of 2018 that quoted insiders at the time, Spiegel refused to believe that the copying was contributing to a slowdown in Snapchat's growth.[25] Spiegel felt so strongly that other factors were at play and his head-strong approach to the design of Snapchat had served him well that he was unable to recognize a grave threat to his business. When Spiegel eventually came to realize that Facebook's copy of the feature was hurting Snapchat, he dismissed the threat offhandedly. In a *Recode* live interview, he said that it might be easy for Facebook to copy a feature, but extremely hard for them to replicate the values of Snapchat, values which in his mind would continuously fuel its ongoing growth.[26] This was a glaring case of overconfidence bias. But don't luxuriate in schadenfreude about Speigel's inanity. We're all vulnerable to this.

This bias has been studied experimentally in the domains of leadership, finance, medicine, and more. The results each and every time show that regardless of the field, all human beings make the mistake of overestimating their skills sometimes, which can have horrifying results. Take the case of overconfidence among physicians.

In a *JAMA Internal Medicine* (a peer-reviewed medical journal published by the American Medical Association) study, 118 doctors from all across the United States were given a total of four cases to diagnose.[27] Two were straightforward and two were relatively more difficult. For each of the four cases, the doctors were given information on the cases in an evolving manner: first the patient's presenting symptoms, then more and more information as the case unfolded. In total, the physicians received four chunks of information for each case. At the end of each information chunk, the doctors were asked what diagnoses they were considering *and* their confidence level in making that diagnosis. The results were sobering. For the easy cases, the physicians were correct in their diagnoses 55 percent of the time. For the difficult cases, this number dropped to 5 percent (accuracy rates in this study are low as the researchers chose somewhat unusual cases). What is surprising, however, is that the doctors' self-reported confidence levels barely differed in relation to the case they were diagnosing. The doctors were as confident in their diagnoses of the difficult cases as they were of the easy cases, even though they were right only 5 percent of the time with the hard cases. As with all of the other biases we've examined, being savvy is about finding the sweet spot in corralling the bias. Confidence up to a certain point is a great thing. But left to run rampant, it clouds critical thinking and muddies our judgment.

It did so with Snapchat's Evan Spiegel when he led a major redesign of the service. The new design allowed users to separate personal messages among friends from professional content from brands and celebrities. Tests showed that users hated it and wanted all the content together as it had been. But even when presented with that data, Spiegel chose to go ahead with the overhaul.

His critics rolled their eyes in disbelief when the changes launched and failed to gain traction with Snapchat's user base. Spiegel continued to argue, as pointed out in the *Businessweek* story, that ignoring critics had served him well. From disappearing stories, which seemed silly at first to most people, to allowing users to turn their faces into bunnies, at every turn, Spiegel explained, he'd been told that his ideas were bad. In his view, ignoring critics was essential to his successes. He said, "Over and over again, everyone told us that our company was going to fail. We worked against all odds, especially in this landscape with tech giants."[28] The more he was criticized, the more he dug in his heels, frustrating employees, board members, and friends rooting for his and Snapchat's success.

Spiegel's overconfidence actually led him to create a company of obeisance. People who have worked with him have said that decision-making at Snapchat worked in a very simple way. You either agreed with Spiegel and allowed him to make all the major decisions or you left the company. It was his company and his personal decision-making process that drove everything at Snapchat. In fact, employees believe that one of the easiest ways to get on Spiegel's bad side was to recommend a solution simply because it had worked elsewhere (exactly the opposite philosophy of Facebook's). Spiegel so wanted to be right. To argue with him put your job at risk. Not surprisingly, SnapChat saw several leaders come and go very quickly, from its Chief Operating Officer, head of product, and head of sales to its head of HR and many talented employees below them.

The story of SnapChat Inc. is still being written. Our hope is that it will take a more positive turn, but that will depend immensely on how much Evan Spiegel learns to listen to the views that conflict with his own.

PAUSE BEFORE SHARING

In 2009, Dr. Deb Roy, an MIT professor, had just started his company Bluefin Labs. The company's mission was to find patterns in social media data to measure viewer engagement with TV shows and advertisements at scale. Until then, it was easy to tell when the TV was on, but much more difficult to determine whether someone was actually in the same room paying attention to it. Using a combination of temporal analysis, semantic examination, and machine learning, the company found ways to solve that problem. Advertisers used Bluefin's analyses many times over to drive much more accurate and efficient media planning, buying, and measurement programs. Bluefin Labs did well and was recognized as one of the 50 most innovative companies of 2012 by *Technology Review* magazine. It was ultimately acquired by Twitter in 2013. Dr. Roy joined Twitter to serve as its chief media scientist.

Forever curious, Dr. Roy left Twitter in 2017 to return to academia full-time, running the Laboratory for Social Machines (LSM) at the MIT Media Lab. The LSM team's mission is to use natural language processing, network science, machine learning, and user experience design to conduct analyses and build tools to promote deeper learning and understanding in human networks. It was the LSM team that made the discovery we introduced earlier that fake news travels around Twitter faster than true news. Entitled "The Spread of True and False News Online" the project was conducted in partnership with Soroush Vosoughi (his PhD student at the time) and Dr. Sinan Aral (another Vosoughi advisor). Inspired by the tragic Boston Marathon bombing of 2013 in the aftermath of which they struggled to discern the differences between real and fake news on Twitter, they set out to develop a model that could predict the accuracy of rumors on the social media platform. Twitter supported the research and provided the team full access to its historical archives for this effort.[29]

The team studied true and false news stories distributed on Twitter over the eleven-year period between 2006 and 2017. Their data set included approximately 126,000 cascades of news stories that were tweeted by about 3 million people over 4.5 million times. Using six independent fact-checking organizations that exhibited a 95–98 percent agreement on the classifications, they classified all the news stories as either true or false.

Source: Twitter.com retrieved on November 30th, 2018

The study found that false news was 70 percent more likely to be retweeted than true news. In all categories, falsehoods diffused significantly farther, faster, and deeper than the truth. True stories take about six times as long to reach the same number of people as do false ones. While the effect was most pronounced for false political news, it also included terrorism, natural disasters, science, urban legends and financial information. Additionally, the spread of false news wasn't driven by bots as we might like to think but rather by human beings. The research showed that bots spread true and false news at a similar rate.

How can so many of us be that devious or unscrupulous? It is understandable that in any social media context bad actors will spread false news. However, such a significant variation in the rate at which false news spreads relative to the truth tells us something else. One factor is that fake news is often perceived as more novel than true news—people want to be the first to share information on social media sites in order to build their own social capital. But a strong factor is that we prefer to spread news that fits with our biased views. In this post-trust era, we may not know what is true, but we do know what we like to believe.

We so deeply want to be right that it is more important to us to have evidence that we are right than it is for the so-called evidence itself to be accurate. In this sense, it has become possible to be both more well-informed and more closed-minded at once. That's a key reason so many of us are active participants in the virality of fake news.

We should all coach ourselves to take good pause before we pass on any bits of scoop we're thrilled about and ask ourselves, why am I so eager to believe this? Is this just making me feel good, or do I really think it's credible? The desire to be right is remarkably powerful, but we can teach ourselves to counteract its allure.

GET SAVVY NOW
RESISTING OUR NEED TO BE RIGHT

- **Ask yourself "what if the opposite was true":** It is not simply enough to ask people to be fair and impartial. Asking them to think about the *opposite* condition to their own conclusions forces them to reflect and it removes bias.

- **Appoint people to play "devil's advocate":** When tasked with making a major decision, set up an alternative team whose responsibility is to justify the opposite conclusion. It will lead you to better solutions.

- **Form non-traditional allies within your company or among business partners and in the media** - people who may not agree with what you do, but respect you and respect the truth even more. It will help remove bias in your own decision making.

- **Be thoughtful and constructive:** Don't state your correction as a negation of the lie. Introduce the contradictory facts in a thoughtful fashion. Use emotion and present the facts in a non-confrontational, constructive manner to have the most impact.

- **Overcome your naive realism:** Just because someone is an expert, doesn't mean they're always right. They can also suffer from cognitive biases like naive realism. Recognize the limits of the experts who are advising you and find ways to counter the biases at play.

- **Recognize your own biases:** Widen the aperture of influences that you are exposed to. Find ways to more accurately determine your true competence in a given subject.

- **Be open to criticism.** Find trusted people who can provide you with feedback in a way where the message is heard without it feeling like an attack. It is important to have people surrounding you who don't agree with everything you say all the time.
- **Admit you are wrong:** If you're a leader, be willing to admit that you're wrong sometimes. The more you project yourself as being self aware, open to alternative viewpoints and willing to change when you're wrong, the more your company will be too.

CHAPTER 5

● ● ● ● ●

WE BOW TO AUTHORITY

"Nothing strengthens authority so much as silence."
— LEONARDO DA VINCI

EICHMANN'S TRIAL

IN 1961, NAZI WAR CRIMINAL ADOLF EICHMANN WAS PUT ON TRIAL IN JERUSALEM FOR WAR CRIMES AFTER HIS CAPTURE IN ARGENTINA. He was held in a fortified police station at Yagur in Israel for nine months while the Israelis interrogated him extensively, hoping to extract a confession. Every time the interrogators trapped him by demonstrating his statements contradicted the evidence they already had, Eichmann would insist that he had no authority and had merely been obeying orders.

When the trial began on April 11, 1961, Eichmann's defense team used the same logic, basing their arguments on the premise that he had no authority in the Nazi hierarchy and was simply following orders.

Throughout his testimony, Eichmann insisted he had been bound by an oath of loyalty to Hitler and was following orders from his chain of command—Müller, Heydrich, Himmler, and ultimately Hitler. The same superior orders defense had been used by some defendants in the 1945–1946 Nuremberg trials. The gist of the defense was that a subordinate is not criminally liable for crimes committed in obedience to the orders of a superior.

Years later when Eichmann's plea for pardon was released to the public, it said, "There is a need to draw a line between the leaders responsible and the people like me forced to serve as mere instruments in the hands of the leaders."[1] He further wrote, "I was not a responsible leader, and as such do not feel myself guilty." The trial later proved that Eichmann did have authority, but his claim not to raised important questions for psychologist Stanley Milgram. As he wrote, "Could it be that Eichmann and his million accomplices in the Holocaust were just following orders? Could they even be called accomplices?" Milgram set out to find the answers in a landmark study whose results he presented in an article published in *Harper's Magazine* in 1973 titled, "The Perils of Disobedience."[2] That article has served as the foundation for how researchers have studied leadership for decades to follow.

ADMINISTERING ELECTRIC SHOCKS

Can you imagine being strapped in an armchair and administered electric shocks simply for not answering a question correctly? What if the voltage of those electric shocks increased with each mistake you made to the point that the shocks became life-threatening? Who would be so cruel as to inflict such punishment? Sadly, most of us. That's the finding at the heart of the widely cited experiments with which Milgram sought to understand how and why people obey commands—even truly heinous ones.

Milgram launched the experiment in July 1961 in the basement of Linsly-Chittenden Hall at Yale University. He wanted to discover how much pain ordinary people would be willing to inflict on others simply because an authority figure instructed them to. In designing the experiment, a bit of deception was employed. Milgram recruited forty male participants via a newspaper ad. They were asked to draw lots to determine who would act as the teacher and who would act as the learner. In reality, some participants were co-conspirators in the study. The drawing of lots was done in a way that ensured the co-conspirators (who were paid actors) would always be the learners. The teachers were the only true guinea pigs in the study and had no idea that the learners were actors.

As you might remember, here's how the study began. An experimenter strapped a learner into an electric chair as the teacher watched and explained for both to hear that this was to prevent the learner from escaping. Next, electrodes were placed on the learner's head. The teacher and the learner were then separated into adjacent rooms so that they could communicate, but not see each other. The teacher was given a list of word pairs that he was to teach the learner. These pairs of words were read aloud to the learner, whose memory was tested by repeating the first word and then mentioning four different options to pair with it. If the learner chose the wrong answer, he would be administered an electric shock. For every wrong answer, the electric shock voltage would increase by 15 volts. The shock generator had thirty switches marked in 15-volt intervals from 15 to 450 volts. Milgram placed warnings on the machine corresponding to the levels of electric shock. The warnings started at "Slight Shock," progressing to "Strong Shock," "Extreme Intensity Shock," "Danger: Severe Shock," culminating with "XXX."

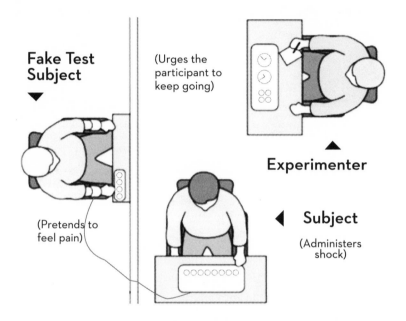

Here is where the study gets fascinating. The teachers thought that every time they administered an electric shock, the learners were, in fact, receiving it. However, the experiment was set up so that no actual shocks were delivered. A pre-recorded tape of the learners' supposed responses to the shocks was played. For the lower-level shocks, the teachers would hear the learners calling out, "I can't stand the pain." With the stronger shocks, the teachers heard the learners screaming in pain and pleading with them to stop administering the shocks. At the highest level, the teachers would hear the learners yelling, "You can't hold me here! My heart's bothering me!"

There was one more piece to the experiment. If at any time the teacher wanted to stop (and asked the experimenter if he could) the experimenter was instructed to give specific responses, in the following order:

- Please continue.
- The experiment requires that you continue.
- It is absolutely essential that you continue.
- You have no other choice; you must go on.

The experiment would be stopped if the teacher refused to continue even after the four verbal prods to carry on. The only other way it would be stopped was if the subject had administered the maximum 450-volt shock three times in succession.

Ahead of the experiment, Milgram surveyed Yale University senior-year psychology students, asking them to predict the behavior of the participants. They all estimated that only a small fraction of the teachers (less than 3 out of 100) would be prepared to inflict maximum damage. Milgram also polled his colleagues who similarly surmised that very few of the teachers would progress beyond strong shocks and would resist the experimenter's nudges to continue. They thought that "only a little over one-tenth of one percent of the subjects would administer the highest shock on the board."

What do you think happened? What would you do if you were asked by an authority figure to administer electric shocks to someone for not answering a multiple-choice question correctly? You're probably thinking that, like most other well-meaning people, your humanity and moral compass would prevent you from conducting such a harsh punishment for forgetting pairs of words. Perhaps.

Shockingly (excuse the pun), Milgram found the opposite to be the case. In his first set of experiments, 65 percent (26 out of 40) of the teachers administered the final massive 450-volt shock, and *all* administered shocks of at least 300 volts. They did not find doing so easy, displaying varying degrees of stress each time they applied the shocks including sweating, trembling, stuttering, biting their lips, groaning, digging their fingernails into their skin, and even having nervous laughing fits or seizures. Every teacher paused the experiment at least once to question it, and many were in obvious distress at critical points. Nonetheless, most continued after being prodded by the experimenter.[3]

The experiments unmasked two startling facts about human nature. The first being that even though people are taught at a young age not to hurt anyone, they quickly push that tenet aside when obeying an authority figure. We are given to following those in power even if they have no material influence whatsoever on our lives. It is as if we're programmed to follow instructions from someone who appears to be in a position of authority regardless of how illogical (or unethical) their commands may be. Second (and worse), we rarely question the source of an authority figure's power. While the study showed that participants struggled with implementing the punishment, they never questioned the experimenter's right to conduct the study.

To quote Stanley Milgram, "Ordinary people, simply doing their jobs, and without any particular hostility on their part, can become agents in a terrible destructive process. Moreover, even when the destructive effects of their work become patently clear, and they are asked to carry out actions incompatible with fundamental standards of morality, relatively few people have the resources needed to resist authority."[4]

Where does this leave us? The Milgram experiment is famous because it underscores the fundamental truth that human beings are pre-disposed to trust people in positions of authority. This helps to explain why deceitful leaders are often able to remain in power: their backers and employees don't oppose their authority even though their ethics are dubious. In fact, there are many instances in which corporate leaders have been deferred to even when glaring warning signs spelled trouble.

WHEN AUTHORITY FIGURES COST US OUR JOBS

Few things are as iconically American as baseball. From singing "Take Me Out to the Ballgame" on a warm summer night to hearing the crack of the bat, shelling peanuts, and cheering on your favorite team, baseball is woven into the fabric of America. It is a classic symbol of Americana and reminder of a wholesome, simpler time.

Yet baseball was anything but wholesome and simple back in July 1999. That's when Richie Phillips, then head of the Major League Umpires Association (MLUA), convinced the majority of umpires in his union to participate in his ill-conceived negotiating ploy. He persuaded fifty seven of his umpires to tender their resignations to the Major League Baseball association (MLB) in an attempt to negotiate a new labor agreement. Phillips told them the league would be unable to replace the umpires on short notice and would concede to their demands. He also banked on the MLB doing everything in its power to avoid handing over $15 million in severance pay. On the surface, it appeared to be a savvy move for the umpires who weren't allowed to strike due to an existing collective bargaining agreement.

But what happened next was completely unexpected. Rather than budging, the league chose to sit on their resignations. The umpires panicked and the majority tried to rescind their resignations. But the league wasn't having it. Suddenly, all of the umpires were without a chance for a new labor agreement and more worrying, twenty-two were without jobs. The MLB had announced its intention to hire twenty-five replacement umpires from the minor leagues.

What had gone wrong? Phillips had miscalculated. He was attempting to bring the MLB to the bargaining table but instead ended up leading his men to commit occupational suicide. The umpires had blindly acted on his advice. They later said that they were led to believe that the resignation letters wouldn't be sent. They also didn't understand the full repercussions of signing the letters. Union membership fractured. Some umpires petitioned to decertify the union and replace it with a new one. Many questioned their union leadership, the information that was being fed to them, and the effectiveness of the organization that was meant to protect their rights.[5] Trust had been broken.

By November 1999, all hell had broken loose. Richie Phillips was ousted by the umpires after more than twenty years at the helm of the

MLUA. The union itself was disbanded and a new association, the World Umpire Association, was formed under fresh leadership and governance. Phillips had made a fatal mistake—he had misled his umpires, obfuscated facts, withheld information, and made a brazen, colossal miscalculation. But the greater mistake was made by the umpires who chose to act on his direction without deliberation. They trusted him blindly. Most did not spend any time evaluating the request to resign, assessing the veracity of the strategy or exploring other less risky options. They argued (just as Adolf Eichmann and the teachers in Milgram's experiment did) that they were simply following directions.[6]

What are the takeaways? First, it can be far easier to follow leaders than to raise objections. But the easy route can come back to bite you. In a world of so much obscurity, we need to depend much more on our own judgment. We must always assess a leader's legitimacy and whether an authority figure is deserving of our respect and followership before committing to him or her. As the saying goes, trust, but verify.

Also, it is easy to blame our leaders. With any scandal in the political or business arenas, we are quick to identify a culprit and squarely place all blame on their shoulders. But they've often taken advantage of our very human (and often very flawed) proclivity to listen to authority figures even if their directions fly in the face of common sense. We need to be aware of our role in aiding authority figures in faulty decision-making and abuse of power. And most critically, once we have that awareness, we need to stand up to untrustworthy authority figures.

In challenging authority, it helps to consider that you're often not alone. No doubt, questioning a leader can be extremely difficult. It may mean putting your job or reputation on the line. Seek out allies to support your case and partner with you. Had those teachers in the Milgram experiment spoken to each other, they may not have gone as far as they did with the electric shocks.

Indeed, Stanley Milgram showed that dissent was easy to orchestrate. In one variation of the study, he had teachers participate in groups of three. Unbeknownst to the actual participant, the other two teachers were actors, with scripts on how and when to dissent. One of the actors was to say that he couldn't go on when the shock reached 150 volts. The other said the same thing when the shock reached 210 volts. With both of the actors refusing to go on, the experimenter made strong efforts to get the third teacher to continue. About nine out of ten people refused to obey under these circumstances. Dissent is contagious. When a few people are brave enough to speak out, it gives other people the courage to do so as well.

And finally, if you are an authority figure, constantly remind yourself that you must earn respect for your leadership, not simply assume it should be bestowed. Otherwise you're in danger of isolating yourself from important input and counterarguments, and of letting your power get the better of you. To assure you get the pushback that can help you avoid bad judgments, you can't assume your subordinates will voluntarily offer it to you: you have to ask for it.

TRAVIS KALANICK AND THE PERILS OF OBEDIENCE

Born August 7, 1976, Travis Kalanick was raised in Northridge, California. He was keenly interested in computers from a young age and learned to write code by the time he was in middle school. He eventually found his way into a computer engineering program at UCLA. Like many famous entrepreneurs before him, Kalanick dropped out of college to work on his startup, Scour, a peer-to-peer search engine. Scour was one of the first dot-com companies to enable users to share music and movies online. The business failed and filed for Chapter 11 bankruptcy after several entertainment companies sued it for copyright infringement to the tune of $250 billion. But that didn't stop Kalanick. He picked himself up by the bootstraps and began work on his next startup, RedSwoosh, another company specializing in file-sharing technology. Kalanick eventually sold RedSwoosh to Akamai for $19 million in 2007.[7] After spending a year traveling around the world, he moved on to his third startup—Uber.

On New Year's Eve in 2008, Garrett Camp (co-founder of Uber) and his friends decided to splurge a little and bring in the new year on a high note. They hired a private driver and spent the night driving around to various parties and hotspots. At the end of the evening, the driver handed them a bill for $800. After forking over the money, Camp and his friends started talking about how there should be a cheaper ride service. They came up with a simple idea: if people *shared* the cost of a ride, it would become more affordable. That was the simple spark behind Uber. Kalanick joined the team soon after the startup was launching.[8]

As a fledgling startup, Uber started with only three cars for hire. It has since grown to have operations in 785 metropolitan areas worldwide and has had a peak valuation of $70 billion. But its explosive growth over nine years isn't what makes Uber interesting for us. It's what Susan Fowler, a software engineer at the company, wrote about on February 19, 2017. In her 3,000-word blog post, "Reflecting on One Very, Very Strange Year at Uber," Fowler outlined the discrimination she had faced at the company, which included being propositioned for sex by a former manager.[9] She further detailed the inaction of Uber's Human Resources department which chose to ignore the issue because the manager in question was a high performer. Human Resources told Fowler to either find another team to work on or figure out a way to work with her existing manager who would give her a bad performance review at the end of the year. Uber was excusing the behavior of its "brilliant jerks" simply because they were high performers.

Fowler's blog post quickly received over 500 comments, more than 14,000 likes and was shared 22,000 times on Twitter. Coverage of the allegations swirled in the mainstream press, setting into motion a series of events at Uber that eventually led to the ousting of founder and CEO Travis Kalanick (officially he resigned). Those events included Uber hiring legal minds to investigate Fowler's concerns as well as harassment claims of other employees. One of those two legal minds was Eric Holder, former US Attorney General. The report published by Holder detailed many examples of sexual misconduct among the Uber employees and their leaders.

Why is this story relevant to the crisis of trust? Because bad behavior at Uber was so widely known by employees, and the higher-ups that could have combated it instead condoned it. The company's culture was abusive long before Fowler joined. Uber was broken and had been for a quite a while. The company's culture was implicitly condoning jerk-like behavior. And driving the company's culture were leaders who carried most of the blame.

One could argue that because Uber was growing so fast, questioning the company's leadership seemed to fly in the face of results. Indeed, it may have seemed that the culture was partly responsible for the great results. But the culture wasn't necessary for strong growth: it emerged from Kalanick's example.

He was a brash and arrogant leader, who thrived on competition and treated it as combat. Kalanick created an environment at Uber that reflected his more extreme tendencies—rewarding the same hyper-competitiveness that was in his DNA and encouraging success at any cost. The Uber mantra at the time was an extreme version of the Silicon Valley startup motto "move fast and break things." Kalanick was determined to move faster, bringing product innovations to market quicker than any of his competitors. His ambitions and drive were impressive, but with them came questionable ethics. Kalanick's mentor Mark Cuban once said that Kalanick's willingness to "run through a wall to accomplish his goals" was both his biggest strength and greatest weakness.[10]

Uber's culture encouraged and celebrated a "take no prisoners" attitude among its employees. Over the years, behaviors included turning a blind eye to sexual harassment charges, spying on passengers, suspicious driverless car experiments in San Francisco, and using illegal software to track regulators. One of the more egregious accusations against Uber is that it tried to take advantage of a situation and do business at John F. Kennedy International Airport during a taxi strike. The strike was to protest Donald Trump's executive order barring travelers from seven majority-Muslim countries from entering the country. This episode led to the popularization of the Twitter hashtag #DeleteUber.[11]

Uber's and Lyft's U.S. market share

Source: Second Measure. *Other includes Gett, Juno, Sidecar and Via

The behavior of Eric Alexander, Uber's former president of Asia Pacific business, is just one example of how Kalanick's leadership resulted in a morally compromised company culture. In December 2014, a twenty-six-year-old woman in Delhi accused her Uber driver of raping her after she dozed off during her ride home. Alexander illegally obtained copies of the woman's medical records and carried them around with him for months, sharing the confidential material with other Uber executives. Alexander was convinced that the rape charges were fake, and that the rape had been set up by Ola, Uber's chief rival in India. He and Kalanick had lengthy discussions on how the woman's records were at odds with her account, serving in their minds as evidence that the rape was a hoax. Neither Alexander nor the other executives to whom he showed the medical records considered turning the documents over to the authorities. It was only after a reporter broke the story that they took responsibility.[12]

How could Travis Kalanick and Uber's experienced management team allow for the culture to turn so sour? What was missing in the equation? Could it all be blamed on Kalanick? Some would argue that Uber, with its thousands of employees, could not have been so thoroughly influenced by one person alone. But there seems little question that the negativity started at the top and eventually seeped into all parts of the organization. Kalanick's direct reports adopted his personality traits and followed in step with his aggressive behavior. Other employees recognized that Kalanick had a problem and that the entire culture of the company had been sullied by his personality, but they dared not raise a red flag.

None of this excuses Kalanick. But it does show that leaders inspire conformity, even to the point where many people are willing to put their decency, moral compass, and ethics aside. If you take a leader like Kalanick and put him in an environment with no checks and balances because everyone is too afraid to disobey him, you have a crisis waiting to happen. As Stanley Milgram summarized the results of his study, "It is not so much the kind of person a man is as the kind of situation in which he finds himself that determines how he will act."

THE ELIXIR OF POWER

We should never underestimate how leaders, of any kind, may be corrupted by power. Another of the most famous—and notorious—studies in the history of psychology demonstrated how readily people can become enamored by, and then abuse, power. Referred to as the Stanford prison experiment, it was conducted in 1971 by Philip Zimbardo.[13] He set up a mock prison at the university to look at the dynamics between people in a leader/servant relationship. Twenty-four sane, middle-class, predominantly white individuals were paid fifteen dollars to participate in the study. The researchers intentionally excluded individuals who had criminal backgrounds, psychological impairments, or medical problems. The basement of the Stanford psychology department was retrofitted to function as a prison with fabricated walls, cells, and cots for the prisoners. Meanwhile, the guards were given much more comfortable living quarters. The study was initially designed for two weeks but was cut short after barely six days as several volunteers began suffering from significant emotional trauma. Here's how it all went down.

Subjects were randomly assigned to either play the role of "prisoner" or "guard." Every effort was made to make the experiment feel as real as possible. The Palo Alto police department "arrested" the prisoners, deloused them, and forced them to wear chains and prison garments. The prisoners were then transported to the basement of the Stanford psychology department.

The researchers held an orientation session for the guards a day before the experiment, at which time they were given sunglasses and sticks. During the orientation, guards were specifically instructed not to physically harm the prisoners or withhold food or drink. In recorded videos of the orientation, Zimbardo was seen telling the guards, "You can create in the prisoners feelings of boredom, a sense of fear to some degree, you can create a notion of arbitrariness that their life is totally controlled by us, by the system, you, me, and they'll have no privacy.... We're going to take away their individuality in various ways. In general, what all this leads to is a sense of powerlessness. That is, in this situation we'll have all the power and they'll have none."

Day one of the experiment started uneventfully, but by the second day, there were signs of trouble. Several of the prisoners blockaded their cell doors, refused to come out, or follow any of the guards' instructions. Guards from other shifts stepped in to help quell the riot using fire extinguishers—the researchers did not approve of this. Recognizing that the prisoners would always outnumber the guards, they resorted to mind games to manage the prisoners. These included privileging prisoners who behaved well with extra benefits and ignoring the others or making them do push-ups as punishment for disobedience. By day three, things had gone from bad to worse, culminating with one prisoner completely losing his composure and starting to scream uncontrollably. This prisoner had to be released from the study early.

With each passing day, the guards struggled to control the prisoners and progressively introduced more sadistic tactics to manage them, especially at night when they assumed the cameras were off. These tactics included forcing some prisoners to urinate or defecate in a bucket placed in their cell and punishing them by not allowing the prisoners to empty the bucket. For disobedience, the prisoners' mattresses were removed forcing them to sleep on concrete. As a further method of degradation, some prisoners were forced to be naked. Ultimately, on day six, the experiment was shut down for fear that one of the prisoners would be seriously hurt. Many of the guards were upset when the experiment was terminated.[14]

The fears that drove the halting of the experiment were shared by Christina Maslach, a graduate student in psychology whom Zimbardo was dating at the time (and later went on to marry). She strongly objected to the conditions of the prison after she was introduced to the experiment to conduct interviews. Interestingly, of the more than fifty people who had observed the experiment, Maslach was the only one who questioned its morality. That too tells us something about human behavior. The title of Zimbardo's book on the subject best captures the experiment: *The Lucifer Effect: Understanding How Good People Turn Evil.*[15]

It is easy to dismiss this study and maybe a few of those mentioned earlier in the book as controlled psychology experiments with no actual bearing on the real world or corporate life. After all, a student prison experiment in an elite institution with twenty-four participants couldn't be further from the goings-on of corporate America. Corporate leaders would never behave that way; they're too intelligent, too moral, too disciplined, and too mature to even move in directions approximating how the sadistic guards behaved. But are they really?

BETWEEN STEVEN SPIELBERG AND GOD

He has been thanked more than almost anyone else in movie history, ranking just after Steven Spielberg and right before God. Over a career spanning more than forty years, he's been a towering influence on Hollywood, considered one of the most dominant people in the century-old history of the industry. He has more successful films to his name than anyone else, more than three hundred Oscar nominations for these films, and is an honorary Commander of the Order of the British Empire. In 2012, he was made a knight of the French Legion of Honor in addition to receiving a Milestone Award from the Producers Guild of America and the British Film Institute fellowship from that organization among other various accolades. Can you guess who he is?

We are talking about none other than Harvey Weinstein. In October of 2017, Weinstein's world came crashing down. In an explosive piece of investigative journalism, a *New Yorker* story discussed the results of interviews with thirteen women who said that Weinstein had sexually harassed or assaulted them.[16] A *New York Times* story from a few weeks earlier included similar allegations, corroborating the premise that Weinstein spent years abusing his position of authority.[17] Other women started stepping forward, sharing their similar experiences with Weinstein. In the end, more than one hundred women had accused him of sexual misconduct.

It is commendable that these women found the courage to speak out against Weinstein. But what is most striking is the fact that so many people knew about Weinstein's indiscretions and remained silent. From the companies he worked for (Disney and The Weinstein Co.) to his large network of Hollywood friends and acquaintances, their silence protected him. People who worked in Weinstein's orbit were so desperate to remain in good stead with the Hollywood mogul that they turned a blind eye to his behavior and remained silent.

Harvey Weinstein's actions epitomize a flagrant abuse of power. Over his career, he perfected his trade, was showered with accolades, and came to believe he was invincible. This is not a new story. The same script was written for Bill Cosby, Bill O'Reilly, Louis C.K., and Andy Rubin who was at Google. In each of these storylines, the protagonist commits his crimes and the bystanders remain silent. But that is not always the case. Sometimes bystanders have the courage to speak up.

THE STORY OF DUKE TRAN

Whistleblowers who disclose information about wrongdoing are often the target of retaliation. From receiving the cold shoulder, being left out of team meetings, and no longer being considered for promotion to risking a pay cut, facing the threat of being demoted or even losing their job, whistleblowers put a lot on the line.

Such is the story of Duke Tran.[18] He worked at Wells Fargo's debt-collections center. On what started out as just an ordinary day at work, Tran's phone rang. Walter Coles, a customer in Lexington, North Carolina was on the other end of the line. Coles was calling about a letter he'd recently received stating that his wife owed the bank nearly $90,000 and that if she didn't pay it within ninety days, the bank would foreclose on their home. This letter was the first time Coles ever heard of the loan. Tran listened to the story and tried to pull up the Coles' file. No matter where he looked, he couldn't find the loan documents. He informed the Coles that the papers were missing.

After hanging up, Tran asked his boss, Peter LeDonne, about the situation. LeDonne instructed Tran not to follow up with the Coles. Instead, if they called back, Tran was to tell them that the $90,000 was a balloon loan—a type of loan that would require the Coles to pay the full amount back to the bank all at once. Tran was distraught about how the Coles' inquiry was being handled. He took his concern to his boss and his boss's boss. Soon after, Tran was called into LeDonne's office. In the room were Tran's superiors. They asked for his security badge and informed him that he was fired. Effective immediately. He was terminated after more than ten years with the bank.

The Duke Tran story has a rare positive twist. Tran sued Wells Fargo in federal court for retaliation. His lawyers claimed that the bank had tried to silence him, and when that didn't work, they fired him. The judge awarded Tran a seven-figure settlement for damages.[19]

As with many of the other business stories we have discussed in this book, the Wells Fargo story is incomplete. The company is trying to engineer a turnaround to become more ethical and trustworthy. According to new CEO Tim Sloan, the San Francisco-based bank has been implementing numerous reforms that have included "fundamental changes" to its organizational structure including sending customers automatic notifications each time a new account is created. It is fair to say that Sloan recognized the magnitude of his challenges when he pledged at the 2018 Wells Fargo annual shareholder meeting, "Rebuilding trust is our top priority."[20]

How much better would the prospects of the company be if they had encouraged courageous employees like Duke Tran earlier and embraced their sense of right and wrong? How much would you rather look back on your own decisions in the face of abusive authority and be able to say you also acted with courage than have to admit you simply succumbed?

A CAUTIONARY TALE FROM THE PHILIPPINES

On December 1, 2018, Human Rights Watch called upon the Duterte administration in the Philippines to drop the "politically motivated" charges against the online news website, Rappler, and its CEO, Maria Ressa.[21] Behind the announcement is the troubling tale of Ressa, a hero in the war on fake news. Here we see the perils of not bowing to authority.

Who is Maria Ressa? A Princeton graduate and Filipino journalist, Ressa built her career as the Jakarta and Manila CNN Bureau chief and later became CNN's lead investigative reporter for South Asia. In January 2012, Ressa launched Rappler, which started as a Facebook page and later expanded to having its own website. Shortly after its founding, Rappler made a name for itself as a staunch critic of the Philippine government. Not surprisingly, the Philippine government had a problem with Rappler.

By way of background, the Philippine President, Rodrigo Duterte, had been waging a vicious war on drugs, encouraging members of the public to kill suspected criminals and drug addicts. According to the Philippine police, less than five thousand people had been killed.[51] Opposition senators, on the other hand, pegged the number as closer to twenty thousand in 2018 alone.[22] Many believed that the war on drugs extended to include enemies of the government. Duterte, who had a reputation as a "man-of-the-people," has been compared to US President

Trump for his rhetoric.[23] Duterte is also known for his ruthless attacks on journalists who reported critically on his drug war. Using social media, Duterte's men would intimidate, harass, and threaten journalists. Some were even imprisoned. Rappler held the government accountable, reporting on its extrajudicial executions and intimidation tactics.

Ressa began probing Duterte's questionable human rights practices, reporting what she saw his administration to be doing. She reported on how Duterte was manipulating Facebook to spread misinformation and intimidate government dissenters.[24] In a country with 97 percent of the population on Facebook, Ressa saw what damage a powerful dictator could do when wielding a social media platform as a weapon. The more she spoke out against the misinformation, the more viciously she'd be attacked, receiving nearly one hundred threatening social media messages an hour at its height. In the spring of 2018, Ressa met Mark Zuckerberg and pleaded with him to directly address the misinformation that was spreading on Facebook. She believed that there were a mere 26 fake accounts influencing 3 million people.[25]

At his annual state of the nation address in July 2018, Duterte hammered away at illegal drugs, corruption, and pollution in the country. He then went on to demonize news organizations in the Philippines and even singled out Rappler as being foreign-owned and problematic. In August, Duterte's Department of Justice followed up by charging Rappler and Ressa with multiple accounts of tax evasion—charges that most believe to be politically motivated and designed to squash independent media. Two days after receiving the 2018 Knight International Journalism award in Washington DC, Ressa returned to the Philippines where she turned herself into the police. She will stand trial and in all probability go to jail on trumped up charges. All because she stood up to a draconian dictator and pushed back on fake news, using the very same tools he was deploying on social media platforms.

This story is still unfolding as we write and Maria Ressa's fate is unknown. We are highlighting this story not to warn you of the risks associated with fighting fake leaders, fake news, or fake companies (governments in this case), but rather to recognize the heroism of those who do. We also included this story to share just how damaging fakeness can be when left unchecked. Just prior to returning to the Philippines, Ressa was interviewed by Kara Swisher on Recode Decode, warning, "Social media has been the fertilizer of democratic collapse in the Philippines, which should be a cautionary tale for the United States."[26]

A promising outcome of stories like Ressa's is that Facebook and other social media platforms are taking steps to minimize the amount of false information that is spread on their platforms. But this gets more challenging when the source of misinformation is a government itself. Especially when the government is attacking independent media. To succeed, it won't be because of the Maria Ressa's of the world alone. It'll be when everyday people around the world confront their own cognitive biases, address the misinformation themselves, and question authority before unconditionally bowing to it.

GET SAVVY NOW
DON'T BOW TO UNJUST AUTHORITY

- **Seek your allies:** Seek out an ally who is willing to join you in opposing questionable leadership. When you have an ally who shares the same values as you, it is much easier to stand up to unjust authority.

- **Engage in active, critical analysis:** Don't leave the thinking to anyone else. You are ultimately responsible for the decisions that impact your life the most. While you may have bad advisors from time to time (as was the case with the MLB umpires), they should have paid more attention to the negotiations themselves.

- **Question morally dubious directives:** Compliance can have a ripple effect. The more one complies with questionable commands, the harder it is to extract oneself from the authority figure's grip. Don't start to comply if you feel uneasy about the commands.

- **Hold bad leaders accountable:** Be judicious about where you place your trust. Assess a leader's credibility, expertise, experience, and integrity. Don't give bad leaders a pass.

CHAPTER 6

● ● ● ● ●

WE BLINDLY TRUST ARTIFICIAL INTELLIGENCE

"The best way to find out if you can trust somebody
is to trust them"
— ERNEST HEMINGWAY

THE FUTURE IS HERE

REGARDING THE ROLE OF TECHNOLOGY IN THE POST-TRUST ERA, WE'VE THUS FAR CONSIDERED ONLY HOW IT HAS HELPED MAKE FABRICATIONS MORE PERSUASIVE AND FASTER-SPREADING. That is only the tip of the iceberg when it comes to issues of trust regarding technology about which the public must be concerned. Rapidly advancing innovations are providing new capabilities that require us to give serious thought to the degree of trust we should place in the companies and governmental bodies that will be deploying them, and in the technologies themselves.

In this chapter, we'll briefly consider prospects for the future by examining a number of examples of applications for emerging technologies. We'll then take a look further into the future—to consider how we can harness emerging technologies to protect ourselves from potential abuses and reflect on the potential dangers of our brilliant machines becoming more brilliant than we are.

You may ask how we can look at the future through the lens of examples. As William Gibson states, "The future is already here, it's just not very evenly distributed."[1] Artificial intelligence (AI), robotics, and the Internet of Things (IoT) are already entering our daily lives; a brave new world of automation is upon us. Robots are delivering packages and take-out food orders in some cities; semi-autonomous driving technology is guiding more and more cars on the roads. Such conveniences are wonderful, but they may come with costs we haven't anticipated. Now is the time to become savvy about what the ever-more automated future will bring.

SOCIAL CREDIT SYSTEMS - PROXIES FOR TRUST?

Can you imagine going online to search for airline tickets to discover you've been blocked from booking any flights? Or being refused business-class train tickets and rooms at the best hotels even if you can afford them? What if your kids were prevented from attending the best private schools or you were barred from applying for some of the best jobs in your profession? What if this was all due to a series of small transgressions you'd made over an extended period of time, such as sending a few controversial tweets, racking up some parking tickets, playing video games when you could have been studying for exams, posting a fake product review online, or smoking in a non-smoking zone? What if there was no one to appeal to for clemency because those in charge of limiting your freedoms were anonymous artificial intelligence robots that weren't programmed to consider your plea?

This dystopian scenario is more realistic than we'd like to think. China has been developing a system for monitoring its citizens' behavior and giving them a social credit rating, comparable to a financial credit score. The aim is to establish a standardized national reputation scale that can be used, as the China State Council reported, to "allow the trustworthy to roam everywhere under heaven while making it hard for the discredited to take a single step." Three dozen pilot versions have been rolled out in cities across China over the last four years.[2]

One of them is Sesame Credit, launched in 2015 and implemented by the ecommerce conglomerate Alibaba through its financial services arm, Ant Financial, in partnership with the Chinese government.[3] Modeled after the FICO scoring system in the United States and Schufa in Germany, it gathers a much wider set of data, including insurance and loan information, payment histories, public documents including official identity reports, financial records, and information that the government collects through its data protection regulation. Additional inputs include the messages of 850 million active users of China's leading messaging app WeChat, and information about people's dating, shopping, and mobility. Data on more than 300 million real-name, registered users and 37 million small businesses that buy and sell on Alibaba Group's marketplaces has been input.

The data is sorted into five categories:

1. **Credit history:** payment history and levels of debt

2. **Fulfilment capacity:** a user's ability to fulfill contractual obligations

3. **Personal characteristics:** the extent and accuracy of personal information

4. **Behavior and preferences:** users' online behavior including website usage

5. **Interpersonal relationships:** the online characteristics of a user's friends

A complex algorithm determines each user's score. The scores range from 350 for lowest trustworthiness to 950 for highest. From 600 upward one can gain privileges, while lower scores will revoke them. The plan is to make all the scores public so that anyone can know at a glance whether someone is trustworthy. The ultimate goal is to rank order every one of mainland China's 1.4 billion people based on data regarding their economic status, social status, and daily behavior, comparing it to a set of behaviors upon which the government looks favorably. Businesses will also be ranked.

The government hopes to launch the system nationwide by 2020. Already, the program has been used to block nine million people with low scores – referred to as trust breakers—from purchasing airline tickets, renting rooms in hotels, using credit cards, and getting certain jobs, as well as blocking their children from attending certain desirable schools. The government is not keeping the system secret. A story on

Beijing News reported, for example, that seventeen people who refused to do their military service in 2016, identified by the system, were barred from enrolling in higher education. In the city of Rongcheng, photos of high scorers are displayed on boards outside the public library and posted around residential communities, with the boards explaining how to win or lose points. Human Rights Watch uses one word to describe the social credit system—*chilling*. The Chinese government sees it very differently although, pronouncing in a recently published public government document, *"Keeping trust is glorious and breaking trust is disgraceful."*[33]

The government professes an admirable rationale for its social credit system, saying it wants to foster a "culture of sincerity" and enhance trustworthiness, hoping to combat widespread problems such as food safety issues and the counterfeiting of products, and to build a more compliant, orderly society. To put it simply, the government and the various companies and agencies behind the social credit score believe the program would limit fakery in companies, leaders, news, and society at large. But at what cost to personal privacy?

Surely those of us living in democracies don't have to worry about being subject to such a system, right? In reality, some components of a social credit score are already in place in the United States, the European Union, Africa, South America, and other parts of Asia. Once an individual opens a line of credit, data is collected to calculate that person's credit score. If you are given a traffic ticket, points go on your driver's license. When you take an Uber, you can rank the driver and he or she can do the same for you. Airbnb rentals are rated, as are businesses of all kinds on Yelp, TripAdvisor, and many other sites. We've quoted critiques of the Uber work culture earlier found on the workplace review site Glassdoor. Imagine if all of this data were linked together in a single database, along with your voting history and information about you from Facebook and Google.

Would you like to be able to check a score based on this data for a lawyer you're thinking of hiring, or for the companies whose internet services you're choosing among? What about for a teenager your child is dating, or for the teachers at your child's school? It's not unfathomable that such a service might become available; after all, it might well be highly profitable. We in the public must demand now that our elected officials put protections in place to prevent creating such a service – or government-run operation – or it might present itself as a fait accompli.

VEHICLES THAT THINK FOR THEMSELVES

As a married couple with children, we take several road trips a year from our home in the outskirts of San Francisco. Whether we're visiting tourist destinations or any of the various vineyards along the California coast, we inevitably wind up spending much of our weekends driving up and down Highway 101. On a recent road trip to Big Sur, we were passed by a white vehicle zooming down the highway. The driver didn't have his hands on the steering wheel and didn't appear to be paying much attention to the road.

That vehicle was a Tesla Model X, one of the first vehicles in the world to have level 2 self-driving capability, as defined by the Society of Automotive Engineers International standard (which classifies a vehicle's automation for automakers). Level 2 is described as the car being able to steer, accelerate and brake in certain circumstances, with the driver required to perform tactical maneuvers, such as responding to traffic signals, avoiding hazards, and changing lanes. Level 2 is described as "hands off," level 3 is described as "eyes off." Level 3 is defined as responsibility for monitoring the driving environment shifting from the driver to the system, with the car driving on its own.

No companies have been approved by federal and state governments to sell level 3 enabled vehicles as yet, though the Tesla autopilot technology is tantalizingly close when it comes to highway driving. It is not functional for driving in the more complex environments of towns and cities. When you're driving on the highway in a Tesla with the autopilot functionality turned on, all you have to do is intermittently touch the steering wheel when notified to let the car know you're paying attention. The steering, accelerating, decelerating, and avoiding of cars moving in and out of your lane are all managed by the system's series of cameras and very powerful computer.

Barely a few years ago, it was hard to imagine a fully autonomous self-driving car; now they're around the next corner. And it is only a matter of time before vehicles will have level 6 automation, which means the car can operate automatically on any road and under any conditions that a human driver could negotiate. Some vehicles will even be built without steering wheels and pedals. On the inside, they will resemble lounges with the seats facing each other—we'll use them to conduct business meetings, or even take long naps, while on road trips. Car servicing will be triggered remotely and the car will navigate to the dealership on its own and return once complete. Our children are nine and seven years old as we write this. It is quite possible that they will never need to drive their own children to soccer games or organize carpools.

Along the way, we'll be placing an increasing amount of trust in the self-driving cars. Today, the prospect of your car shepherding your loved ones around entirely on its own may seem absurd to you. If so, you're not alone. In a study conducted by AAA in April 2018, 63 percent of Americans said they wouldn't trust riding in a driverless car.[4] But that was down from 78 percent in a 2017 study. Many experts on the technology consider the advent of the fully self-driving era inevitable. A great deal of consideration of the implications and crafting of regulations is needed, starting right now. Who will be accountable when your vehicle gets into an accident with another self-driving car if there were no cameras to capture the event? What if your vehicle gets into an accident with one being manually driven? Should the police and insurers blame the technology or the human driver? We must begin wrestling with these knotty questions.

Adopting increasingly automated cars will involve putting our trust not only in the technology but in the companies creating it. Consider a service automatically provided by Tesla to its drivers when Hurricane Irma hit Florida in September of 2017. A Category 5 storm, Irma was one of the strongest on record to hit the open Atlantic region, leaving more than 7.7 million homes and businesses, approximately 73 percent of those in the state, without electricity at some point. More than sixty-five thousand structures were damaged at a total cost of $50 billion.

Meteorologists saw Hurricane Irma coming, and a few days prior to landfall, Governor Rick Scott declared a state of emergency, ordering an estimated 6.5 million Floridians to evacuate their homes. To assist with the evacuation, Scott also suspended charges on all toll roads in Florida. Tesla decided to step in and help as well.

The company pushed out a software update to all the Tesla vehicles in the evacuation zone that increased their battery capacity. Tesla did this at no cost to the vehicle owners. The cars had latent additional battery power built in, but these customers hadn't paid for the optional extra power when they purchased their cars. The batteries reverted to their standard driving range on September 16, by which time the evacuation was completed.[5]

That was an impressive display of customer service. But now consider that Tesla could just as easily decrease battery range, or perhaps even stop cars from operating altogether, or in the future of full autonomy, instruct them to self-drive to a particular location. That capability could be put to many great uses. Imagine someone stole your car, and you informed the police and Tesla. Before the police even put out a call to search for the car, Tesla could trigger the vehicle to engage autonomous driving, lock the doors and steer the thief to the nearest police station! Or what if the government required Tesla to take control of your car if you are deemed to be driving dangerously? What if nefarious actors figure out how to hack into Tesla's software system and start controlling not only your car but a whole fleet of Teslas around the country?

With each advance in the capabilities of our artificially intelligent creations, new risks will be introduced. AI is not foolproof in part because the humans designing it are not foolproof. Instances of AI going wrong are many. Recall the Google algorithm classifying people of color as gorillas, or when Teslas, operating in autopilot mode, resulted in a fatal accident. As AI becomes more prevalent in our lives, so too will these cases of it failing us. We must begin weighing the benefits against the potential costs now, through vigorous scenario planning. Plenty of cautionary tales of unforeseen consequences can already be told if we blindly trust artificial intelligence.

THE SYSTEM FIRED ME

Ibrahim Diallo was fired by a machine in Los Angeles in the summer of 2017. One day his security pass suddenly stopped working and he was locked out of the corporate computer system. Shortly after, he was frog-marched out of his office building by security personnel. His managers watched in horror. They did not want him fired. He was only eight months into a three-year contract and was doing very good work. When they alerted the higher-level management, they too were mystified.

The system had sent out an email setting the firing in motion. Diallo was later shown the message and recalls, "It was soulless and written in red…. Disable this, disable that, revoke access here, revoke access there, escort out of premises, etc. The system was out for blood and I was its very first victim."

The company eventually figured out that a previous manager Diallo had worked for had forgotten to renew his contract, and the programming of the system automated the firing process in that event, not allowing for human intervention. Diallo eventually got his job back, but the episode raises alarms.[6]

Imagine if instead of one employee being fired, an entire factory or hospital system was closed. The electricity in a whole town could be shut off, or even worse, a military weapon could be mistakenly discharged. With elaborate automated systems, one small error, whether by human or computer, can lead to catastrophe.

We might think the fully automated future is a sure thing, and that we in the public can do little to determine how it unfolds. But for those of us in democracies, we don't have to simply take it as it comes. We can assert our rights and exercise great influence over the companies crafting the technology and our government's regulation of it. We mustn't blindly trust artificial intelligence.

NOT SO FAST, MR. MODI

On November 8, 2016, Prime Minister Narendra Modi announced to the 1.2 billion people living in India in an unscheduled live television address at 8 p.m. Indian Standard Time that 85 percent of the country's cash currency would be taken out of circulation starting at midnight that evening. New 500 and 2,000 rupee notes would be issued in exchange for the old 500 and 1,000 bank-notes. Modi explained that the radical measure was intended to rid the country of "black money" (money that was illegally obtained or not declared taxable), to remove cash that was financing terrorism and to jump start a conversion to a cashless society. He argued the more people who used electronic forms of currency, primarily credit and debit cards and payment apps, the less corruption there would be in the system. The rationale was that electronic currency can be more easily tracked, taxed, and protected. In a later radio address, Modi called upon India's youth to teach ten families a day how to conduct cashless transactions through debit/credit cards and mobile banking.[7]

The Indian public was having none of it. People rushed to with-draw cash while they could, with long queues forming at ATMs and bank branches, causing violence that led to several deaths. Instead of installing new point of sale terminals and aggressively requesting digital forms of payment, many merchants chose to continue their dependence on cash. Consumers who were encouraged to sign up for new credit cards and download and activate mobile money applications did so only in relatively small numbers. After increasing somewhat in December, digital transactions actually declined from January 2017 onward. Cash shortages across the country began to limit business dealings. This led to an economic downturn that was especially acute in the all-important agriculture sector (which accounts for approximately 50 percent of the total workforce in the country). Farmers were intent to stick with cash. Industrial output declined; meanwhile, corruption didn't decrease. While bankers and international commentators had initially supported the move, they'd changed their minds.[8]

The Prime Minister's vision for a cashless society was bold, and that system would likely help a good deal with stamping out corruption. But the people did not trust the government enough to make the switch, and the early difficulties in getting cash out compounded that skepticism. Sure, the corruption problem was widely understood, but, as the saying goes, a known enemy is better than an unknown friend. Democratic governments, and companies that operate in democracies, cannot force the public to embrace technological innovations. The Indian public was perfectly justified in questioning whether the cashless system Modi was touting was adequately protected, and all of us in the public—in the

US and around the world—can and should demand more information about the security of the new automated systems being developed and the uses to which they might be put.

Innovation is not simply by definition for the good, nor is adoption of new technologies and devices simply inevitable. At one point, nuclear power seemed like the breakthrough solution to the ills of fossil fuels. But its potential dangers, and public protests, put a damper on the growth of the industry. An engaged public can bend the arc of the future toward its needs and desires, and the time for engagement is *now*. While the course of technological innovation is not inevitable, in the brave new artificially intelligent era we're entering, if innovators are allowed too much free rein for long enough, the course of development may well escape our control.

WHEN MACHINES BECOME MORE THAN HUMAN

AlphaGo and Lee Sedol challenged some of the most fundamental assumptions of artificial intelligence experts when they played a five-game match of Go on March 9, 2016. Here's the story and why it matters to us.

Go is a Chinese strategy board game, invented more than 2,500 years ago. Played between two players, the goal of the game is to surround more territory on the board with your stones than your opponent does with his. If one of your stones is surrounded by your opponent's stones, it is removed, and play proceeds until there are no more moves to play. The game is more complex than chess. While in chess there are 20 possible opening moves, in Go, there are 361. Go also has many more potential moves per turn. It has a cult following in many parts of East Asia, with roughly 40 million people playing the game. People play Go for hours on end on street corners, in cafes, in their homes, and in the hallowed halls of competition venues.

AlphaGo is a computer program built by researchers at DeepMind, an AI Lab owned by Google. In early March of 2016, it played a five-game match against the South Korean professional player and national hero, Lee Sedol. At the time, Lee was one of the world's best players, carrying a 9-dan ranking (the highest level). He had the second-highest number of Go international victories in the world. Would AlphaGo be able to beat him?

Going into the games, Sedol was confident of winning. On a number of occasions in the months leading up to the match, Sedol stated that he expected to win either all five games or at least four of the five.[9] His confidence wasn't too surprising considering the fact that Go is such a complex game. In fact, in 1965 when asked about the possibility of a Go computer program playing proficiently, mathematician I.J. Good wrote,

"In order to programme a computer to play a reasonable game of Go, rather than merely a legal game—it is necessary to formalize the principles of good strategy, or to design a learning programme. The principles are more qualitative and mysterious than in chess, and depend more on judgement. So I think it will be even more difficult to programme a computer to play a reasonable game of Go than of chess."[34]

As Lee entered the game room at the Four Seasons Hotel in Seoul, most of South Korea was tuning in to the match. An additional sixty million people in China were watching. And for the Western world, the match was being live-streamed on YouTube. Lee sat down across from Aja Huang, one of AlphaGo's programmers, who would see AlphaGo's moves on a computer monitor and then physically move the pieces on the game board accordingly.

Minutes into game 1, Lee became painfully aware of the strength of his opponent. AlphaGo was aggressive and instigated complicated fighting positions. Lee lost the game, resigning after 186 moves. After the first game, Lee said that AlphaGo made one unusual and ingenious move early on that he believed no human Go player would have made. The next day, during game 2, Lee tried a different strategy, holding back and waiting for the computer to make a move he could exploit. AlphaGo made an unexpected play at move 37, a move which commentators have described as both "creative and unique." The move unnerved Lee to the point where he stood up and walked out of the room. Though it was a closer game, Lee ultimately resigned after 211 moves. At the end of game 2, Lee said, "Yesterday, I was surprised. But today I am speechless.

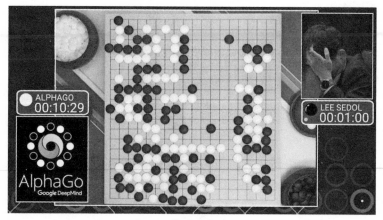

Source: ShellyPalmer.com

The third game was monumental. AlphaGo not only won the game decisively, it played so well that many analysts found its capabilities scary.

Lee did make a comeback to win game 4 when AlphaGo made a critical mistake at move 78. That move happened at a point when analysts watching the game believed AlphaGo had a 70 percent chance of winning, and some likened it to becoming overconfident. The program came booming back in game 5, crushing Lee. South Koreans were shocked. Jeong Ahram, the lead Go correspondent for the Joongang Ilbo, one of the country's biggest daily papers, captured the people's mood well the next morning speaking on the news about the loss when he said, "Last night was very gloomy. Many people drank alcohol."[10]

Google co-founder and Alphabet President Sergey Brin, who had flown in to Seoul especially to watch the series-clinching game, said to *New Scientist* magazine afterward, "AlphaGo actually does have an intuition. It makes beautiful moves. It even creates more beautiful moves than most of us could think of."[11]

Some analysts argued that the program is not only extremely intelligent but has human-like emotions, which has been thought would always be impossible for machines. The capacity for emotion has been considered the final frontier separating human beings from computers. Now that premise is in question. Some AI experts are concerned that we are witnessing the beginning of the end of human mastery over machines, warning that our computers may be becoming superhuman. In March 2016, Stuart Russell, AI researcher at UC Berkeley stated, "AI methods are progressing much faster than expected, (which) makes the question of the long-term outcome more urgent." He added, "In order to ensure that increasingly powerful AI systems remain completely under human control...there is a lot of work to do."[12]

While some innovators, such as Tesla's Elon Musk, are warning about the dangers, others continue to argue that all advances should be commercialized as quickly as possible. Which camp are you in? Do you believe you and the rest of the public are well enough informed about the risks?

We're not arguing that work on AI should be halted. We are arguing that the global public, our governments, and the innovators themselves must not simply trust that all will be well. Some thoughtful recommendations have been made about how we can protect ourselves from AI getting out of our control. Elon Musk believes the human mind should be merged with artificial intelligence, connecting the human brain to computers, so that we become superhuman before our technology does. He has co-founded a startup to explore the possibilities.

James Wilson, co-author of the book, *Human + Machine: Reimagining Work in the Age of AI* proposes guidelines for us to work safely and effectively with artificial intelligence. The human role, he argues, is threefold: (1) training, (2) explaining, and (3) sustaining solutions.[13]

We must train AI technology to do precisely what we want it to do. We can, for example, train our brilliant machines to understand empathy. Imagine if an AI-controlled robot was giving you a piece of bad news, maybe about a medical procedure. You'd want it to do so with compassion. Koko, an MIT startup, has developed a technology for teaching that; you could say Koko is about giving the Tin Man a heart.

Explanation involves human experts in AI illuminating to non-experts how particular applications work. To revisit the case of an accident involving an autonomous car, the human explainer would detail to those assessing liability what the vehicle's capabilities are and the actions it took in the moments leading up to, during, and after the accident.

The job of sustaining entails working with AI systems to continuously ensure they are functioning properly, safely, and responsibly. For example, human sustainers would watch to make sure that an AI system didn't develop any biases over time, which might involve approving credit card applications or mortgage loans for one demographic group more readily than for others.

We will need to develop ethical, humane, and safe solutions for applying AI, and we absolutely can do so. We by no means have to be techno-pessimists. Personally, we could not be more enthused about the power of emerging technologies to enhance people's lives in so many amazing ways. It's how technologies are developed and deployed that will make the difference between dystopia and measured, well-regulated progress. To make the case for trustworthy innovation, let's turn to a story of how brilliantly innovations can be applied to defend against the looming dangers.

IS BLOCKCHAIN THE FUTURE OF TRUST?

In a seminal paper for *The Journal of Cryptography* in 1991 titled, "How to Timestamp a Digital Document," Stuart Haber and W. Scott Stornetta foresaw a future in which all text, audio, picture, and video documents were digitized and easily modified, which was remarkable given that in 1991 there was no World Wide Web and the internet was a little-known technology used mostly by research institutions and the military. They proposed a system that would time-stamp documents in a way that prevented them from being tampered with or backdated.[14]

In a follow-up paper, Haber and Stornetta, along with David Bayer, introduced a refinement to their proposed system whereby several documents would be collected into what they called a block, and the data in any specific block could not be altered retroactively without alteration of all subsequent blocks. The process of creating blocks would be managed by a peer-to-peer network of computer users, and to protect the integrity of each block, all additions were to be propagated across multiple computers in the network in real-time.[15] With that, the foundations of blockchain technology were established, allowing for the creation of what an article in the *Harvard Business Review* (early 2017) described as "an open, distributed ledger that can record transactions between two parties efficiently and in a verifiable and permanent way."[16] The bitcoin currency system is one such ledger.

The mysterious (and still anonymous) Satoshi Nakamoto created the "cryptocurrency" in 2008. Bitcoin is a digital currency that is not managed by a central bank. Funds can be sent among users on the peer-to-peer currency system without the need for any intermediaries, with the blockchain being a public ledger of all bitcoin transactions. All bitcoin transactions are time-stamped and then put into blocks and distributed across all computers in the network. By the end of December 2017, the ledger had grown to a massive 149 GB in size.

Bitcoin is extremely interesting in its own right—scores of journalists, academics and consultants have written about the cryptocurrency and how it will shape our future. But blockchain technology has many additional applications. It can be used to make a wide variety of technologies trustworthy.

To portray its potential to make systems reliable and transparent, the October 2015 edition of *The Economist* magazine looked to Honduras.[17] An article explained how one day in 2009, Mariana Catalina Izaguirre, who had lived in her house in Tegucigalpa for three decades, was suddenly evicted. Even though she had an official title to the land on which the house stood, the country's Property Institute showed another person registered as its owner. That person convinced a judge to sign an eviction order, and by the time the dust from the legal confusion had settled, Ms. Izaguirre's house had been demolished.

Housing records are far from foolproof, not only in Honduras. They can be mismanaged or fall prey to corrupt practices that regular computer systems cannot prevent because digital files can be destroyed or written over. Enter a blockchain solution. The Honduran government asked Factom, an American startup, to provide a prototype of a blockchain-based land registry that no one would be able to tamper with. Once a transaction was recorded in it and propagated across the network of computers, it would be impossible to erase or alter the record. Honduras is just one of many countries that have explored using blockchain technology to manage property records.

The potential uses of the technology are infinite. In the legal profession, validating the existence or possession of signed documents can be done using the blockchain. The movement of money between banks across international borders can be managed with complete safety. In the shipping industry, the movement of goods can be much better tracked. In the luxury goods and pharmaceutical professions, which deal with rampant counterfeiting, blockchain can be used to validate the authenticity of products. Or in the case of fine wine, the legitimacy of each bottle of a particular vintage from a luxury chateau could be determined. With the current system, a bottle is usually sold from the producer to a collector via a series of intermediaries, with the collector then often selling it onward. Tracking the bottle, and whether it is an original or a counterfeit, becomes difficult. A blockchain ledger would provide anyone interested in a given bottle access to its complete ownership trail.

THE NEXT FRONTIER

Blockchain gives us hope that additional brilliant approaches to making intelligent machines trustworthy will be devised. That may not happen, though, unless the public demands it. As of now, we are putting great faith in technology companies. You only need to look at the *Forbes* ranking of the world's most valuable brands to see this. Six of the top ten brands are technology firms. We love the capabilities they're bringing us, as well we should. But new technologies are poised to transform virtually every aspect of our lives, and, as the saying goes, with great promise comes great responsibility.

With technological innovation advancing so rapidly, we're already facing deeply perplexing questions, and the rules of trust for the emerging automated era are just beginning to be written. To be savvy participants in the unfolding story, we must not sit back and trust that others will assure smart choices are made; we need to stay on top of developments and join in the process of writing the new rules of responsibility.

GET SAVVY NOW
BE JUDICIOUS IN TRUSTING AI

- **Use Technocognition:** Technocognition is the idea that we should use what we know about psychology to design technology in a way that minimizes the impact of misinformation.

- **Focus on building trust first:** For technology to gain mass adoption, it requires trust. If you're introducing a new technology, establish a strong foundation of trust among the people whom you want to adopt it.

- **Build faith in AI by explaining how it works:** We can learn to trust AI by becoming more familiar with AI solutions and understanding how they work.

- **Incentivize teams to minimize biases in tech:** Human beings need to manage our biases so that we can orient ourselves toward the truth. In the same way, AI needs to be programmed so as to minimize its biases.

- **Have a neutral arbiter of facts:** Develop a clear understanding of for whom and how the AI technology was developed. Beware the potential dangers of bias and inaccuracies.

- **Make tradeoffs thoughtfully:** New technologies can bring immense benefits to society including helping us form and sustain more trusted relationships with each other. However, the trust benefits may compromise our privacy. Be aware of those tradeoffs.

CONCLUSION

• • • • •

It is difficult to conclude this book. We are tempted to analyze a few more recent egregious examples of fakery. We'd love to tell the story of how The White House revoked (and later restored) the press privileges of CNN correspondent Jim Acosta after falsely accusing him of placing a hand on a young woman based on a doctored video clip from Infowars, a far-right conspiracy website.[35]

We'd like to dive into the case of e-cigarette manufacturer Juul Labs, which the Federal Drug Administration clamped down on for marketing addictive e-cigarettes to minors using social media. While Juul shut down its Facebook and Instagram accounts, and said it would limit the sale of its more teen-friendly flavors in the US, it denied culpability and looked to expand into Indonesia, which doesn't impose penalties for selling cigarettes to minors.[1]

Then there's the recent Brazil presidential election, in which WhatsApp became "an impenetrable candyland of misinformation" according to *Businessweek*. In a two month period, users flagged 60,000 examples of fake news spreading on the platform. One candidate even went so far as to claim that 400 million Brazilians live in extreme poverty though Brazil has a population of only 209 million.[2]

But of course, if we left the door open, the examples would just keep flooding in. And the point of the book is not to chronicle the fakery, but to highlight that it has become a pervasive fact of life in the post-trust era and offer ways for each of us to contend with this reality. That is why we have focused on the ways in which the human mind operates.

We have wanted to illuminate the reasons we fall under the spell of fakery in order to instill a new way of thinking about how to consume and analyze information, and to confer our trust. We've wanted to inspire the desire to be vigilant with ourselves about why we are putting our trust in certain claims, in media sources we prefer, in government figures we champion, or in business leaders we lionize, and why we distrust others. We hope we have encouraged you to step out of your comfort zone and challenge your own views, but also to bring a new perspective to why those you disagree with believe what they do, and how they (like any of us) may be under the sway of manipulation. They may not consciously *want* to believe untruths any more than you do.

Fakery cannot deceive us, or divide us for long if we are not receptive to it. We can build new bridges of trust, even across chasms of hostility, by becoming more savvy about the ways to spot and combat fabrications and distortions.

We began the book by saying that we are optimists. We believe in the power of human goodness to overcome the lesser angels of our nature. We also believe that we can make the world we leave for the next generation better than the one we inherited. Reestablishing a foundation of trust is the bedrock of that brighter future, allowing us to come together to focus on solving pressing problems rather than pointing fingers and flinging accusations. That trust must be built on a basis of understanding. We hope *Savvy* has helped in a small way to empower you and others to assist in making the post-trust era a short-lived episode in the longer story of human progress, one that we and our children look back on from a new grounding of well-founded trustworthiness.

Thank you for reading and visit us at www.savvymatters.com to continue the conversation!

ACKNOWLEDGEMENTS

THIS BOOK WOULD NEVER HAVE BEEN WRITTEN HAD IT NOT BEEN FOR many people who helped us along the way. While we cannot mention everyone, there are a few that we'd like to draw special attention to.

First and foremost, we would like to thank our two sons, Arjan and Shyam, for being such good sports. There have been many a family moment when we should have been talking to them but took the time to squeeze in a book meeting between ourselves. We even made them listen to the occasional TED Talk on the road as we researched for the book. We do hope they retain some of that information!

Our parents and siblings have been rocks for us throughout our lives, and with the book it was no different. From encouraging us to dive into book writing, listening to us as we bounced ideas off of them, encouraging us to persevere when we were tired and reading early drafts of the manuscript, they've been there for us at every stage in the journey. Thank you.

Rohit and the team at Ideapress Publishing have been exceptional. They've brought a high touch, author friendly, personalized experience to the publishing process that is unique. Their thoughtfulness, care and patience is much appreciated. The same goes for our editor, Emily Loose, who did such constructive editing with the manuscript. This book wouldn't be what it is today without her.

Our friends here in Burlingame, California and around the world have been early advocates. They believed in the potential before anyone else did and were patient as we turned dinner party conversations into the occasional discussion of the post-trust era. We like to believe they enjoyed those too but we aren't so sure.

And finally, this book wouldn't have happened had it not been for our professional mentors, friends and workplace peers who shared research articles, read the odd chapter and nudged us along as we labored with the words on the page. Some of them took the time to read early manuscripts end to end and even endorse the book. For others we've simply had the privilege to have worked for or with. That alone has served as inspiration for us as we discussed what is right in the media, among leaders and within companies. To them all, we'll be ever grateful.

RESOURCES

● ● ● ● ●

A FEW ORGANIZATIONS COMBATING FAKENESS

- **First Draft News:** First Draft News is a global coalition of journalism, human rights, and technology organizations dedicated to improving reporting standards and online information. They undertake practical journalism projects in the field to research effective methods for tackling misinformation and disinformation online. They provide ethical guidance on how to find, verify, and publish content sourced from the web. (https://firstdraft-news.org)

- **Google News Initiative:** This initiative strives to establish a working group with news organizations and experts globally to help journalism thrive in the digital age. They are committed to strengthening quality journalism, evolving business models to drive sustainable growth, empowering news organizations through technological innovation, and training journalists.

(https://newsinitiative.withgoogle.com)

- **Internews:** Internews works to ensure access to trusted, quality information that empowers people to have a voice in their future and to live healthy, secure, and rewarding lives. They envision a world where everyone can communicate freely with anyone, anywhere, and exchange the news and information they need to shape their communities and the world. Internews was launched 35 years ago and is in more than 100 countries. (https://www.internews.org/)

- **The Journalism Trust Initiative:** Founded by Reporters without Borders and its partners, this is a voluntary, leading benchmark of media self-regulation and good practices for all those who produce journalistic content, ranging from individual bloggers to international media groups. (https://ethicaljournalismnetwork.org/rsf-trust-initiative)

- **Media Manipulation Initiative (MMI):** The Media Manipulation Initiative examines how different groups use the participatory culture of the internet to turn the strengths of a free society into vulnerabilities, ultimately threatening expressive freedoms and civil rights. Through empirical research, MMI identifies the unintended consequences of socio-technical systems and tracks attempts to locate and address threats, with an eye toward increasing organizational capacity across fields so that action can be taken as problems emerge. (https://datasociety.net/research/media-manipulation/)

- **News Integrity Initiative:** The News Integrity Initiative at the Craig Newmark Graduate School of Journalism at the City University of New York is a fund supporting efforts to connect journalists, technologists, academic institutions, non-profits, and other organizations from around the world to foster informed and engaged communities, combat media manipulation, and support inclusive, constructive, and respectful civic discourse. (https://www.journalism.cuny. edu/centers/tow-knight-center-entrepreneurial-journalism/ news-integrity-initiative/)

- **Trust & News Initiative:** The Reporters' Lab is a center for journalism research in the Sanford School of Public Policy at Duke University. Its projects focus on fact-checking, but it also conducts occasional research examining trust in the news media.

- **The Trust Project:** The Trust Project, a consortium of top news companies led by award-winning journalist Sally Lehrman, is developing transparency standards that help you easily assess the quality and credibility of journalism. (https:// thetrustproject.org/)

A FEW SOFTWARE PLATFORMS FIGHTING FAKE NEWS

- **Civil:** Civil is a self-governing marketplace where citizens directly sponsor newsrooms and journalists collaboratively run their own publications. Their mission is to help power sustainable journalism throughout the world. To do so, they're employing a decentralized model based on blockchain and cryptoeconomics. (https://civil.co/)

- **Crisp Thinking:** Crisp is a leading provider of social media brand safety and crisis monitoring services to global brands, media publishers and social platforms. Crisp has been protecting hundreds of globally recognized brands and social platforms for over ten years, including the world's largest media and entertainment business, four of the top five luxury and fashion brands and the world's largest pharmaceutical company. (https://www.crispthinking.com/)

- **Digital Shadows:** Digital Shadows provides insight into an organization's external digital risks and the threat actors targeting them. Digital Shadows SearchLight™ service combines scalable data analytics with human analysts to monitor for cyber threats, data leakage, and reputation risks. Digital Shadows continually monitors the Internet across the visible, deep and dark web, as well as other online sources to create an up-to-the minute view of an organization and provide it with tailored threat intelligence. (https://www.digitalshadows.com)

- **Factmata:** An artificial intelligence company for automated content scoring and verification, targeting the proliferation of fake and misleading news. The startup aims to be a cross between Wikipedia and Quora, with a community of users fact-checking or marking news articles for quality with the help of AI. Those users may include everyday internet users but also journalists. The company is building a news aggregator designed to show a quality score and offer extra links for context. (http://www.factmata.com)

- **NewsGuard:** NewsGuard addresses the fake news crisis by hiring dozens of trained journalists as analysts to review the 7,500 news and information websites most accessed and shared in the United States. NewsGuard will license its ratings and Nutrition Labels to the various social media and search platforms and other aggregators of news and information so that they can offer the ratings and Nutrition Labels with their feeds. (https://newsguardtechnologies.com/)

- **Our.News:** makes it easy to fact-check any news or digital content, and participate in validating the news using our Open News Validation process. Their mission is to enable the public to separate fact from fiction, to identify the most trustworthy publishers, and judge for themselves what's factual, well-reported and unbiased—and what isn't. Users get all the data, statistics, information and tools they need to quickly determine the truth of any news article, and can then rate any news story for spin, trust, accuracy and relevance. Patent-pending algorithms minimize bias and stop trolls. Aggregate quality scores are then provided for each news story. (https://our.news/)

A FEW FACT-CHECKING WEBSITES

- **FactCheck.org:** Non-partisan, non-profit "consumer advocate" that aims to reduce level of deception in US politics. They monitor the factual accuracy of claims made by politicians via television ads, debates, speeches, interviews, and news releases. (https://www.factcheck.org)
- **OwlFactor:** Automatically calculates the quality of an article based on four factors: the extent and quality of its sources, the expertise of the journalist in the article's topic, the opinionated nature of the article's writing style and the historical scores of articles on the site. This machine-driven calculation means criteria are consistently applied across articles and sources.

(https://www.owlfactor.com/)

- **PolitiFact.com:** Non-profit, non-partisan website dedicated to fact-checking journalism to give citizens information they need to govern themselves in a democracy. (https://www. politifact.com)
- **Snopes.com:** Developed in 1994, Snopes is one of the first online fact-checking websites. The website is deemed a well-regarded source for validating or debunking urban legends and claims made on the Internet . (https://www.snopes.com)
- **TruthOrFiction.com:** A fact-checking website dedicated to unbiased fact checks of news, viral content, and social media. Designed to be of value to the ordinary user of the Internet who wants to make sure that a story contains information, not misinformation. (https://www.truthorfiction.com)

ENDNOTES

INTRODUCTION

1. Charles. *By the King, a Proclamation to Restrain the Spreading of False News and Licentious Talking of Matters of State and Government.* Printed by the Assigns of John Bill and Christopher Barker ..., 1985.

2. *Publick Occurrences, Both Forreign and Domestick. Boston, Thursday, Sept. 25, 1690.* S.n., 1922.

3. Murteira, Helena. "The Lisbon Earthquake of 1755: the Catastrophe and Its European Repercussions." *Lisbon Pre 1755 Earthquake*, 8 June 2016, lisbon-pre-1755-earthquake.org/en/the-lisbon-earthquake-of-1755-the-catastrophe-and-its-european-repercussions/.

4. Soll, Jacob, et al. "The Long and Brutal History of Fake News." *POLITICO*, POLITICO, 18 Dec. 2016, www.politico.com/magazine/story/2016/12/fake-news-history-long-violent-214535.

5. Wilkerson, Marcus M. *Public Opinion and the Spanish-American War: a Study in War Propaganda.* Louisiana State University Press, 1932.

6. Palmier, Leslie. "The 30 September Movement in Indonesia." *Modern Asian Studies*, vol. 5, no. 01, 1971, p. 1., doi:10.1017/s0026749x00002821.

7. Vosoughi, Soroush, et al. "The Spread of True and False News Online." *Science*, American Association for the Advancement of Science, 9 Mar. 2018, science.

sciencemag.org/content/359/6380/1146.

8. "Word of the Year 2016 Is... | Oxford Dictionaries." *Oxford Dictionaries | English*, Oxford Dictionaries, en.oxforddictionaries.com/word-of-the-year/word-of-the-year-2016.

9. ARIELY, Dan. *Predictably Irrational: the Hidden Forces That Shape Our Decisions*. Harper Collins, 2008.

CHAPTER ONE

1. "Address to the General Assembly Secretary-General." *United Nations*, United Nations, www.un.org/sg/en/content/sg/speeches/2018-09-25/address-73rd-general-assembly.

2. "2018 Edelman TRUST BAROMETER." *Home*, www.edelman.com/trust-barometer.

3. "Reuters Institute For the Study of Journalism Releases 2018 Digital News Report; Topics Include Trust, Misinformation, New Platforms, and New Business Models." *LJ InfoDOCKET*, www.infodocket.com/2018/06/14/reuters-institute-for-the-study-of-journalism-releases-2018-digital-news-report-topics-include-trust-misinformation-new-platforms-and-new-business-models/.

4. Kruglanski, Arie W., and E. Tory. Higgins. *Social Psychology Handbook of Basic Principles*. Guilford Press, 2007.

5. Deutsch, Morton. *The Resolution of Conflict: Constructive and Destructive Processes*. Yale University Press, 1977.

6. Berg, Joyce, et al. "Trust, Reciprocity, and Social History." *Games and Economic Behavior*, vol. 10, no. 1, 1995, pp. 122–142., doi:10.1006/game.1995.1027.

7. Jain, Swati. "Travel - The Village with No Locks or Doors." *BBC News*, BBC, 31 May 2016, www.bbc.com/travel/story/20160526-the-village-with-no-locks-or-doors.

8. Granville, Kevin. "Facebook and Cambridge Analytica: What You Need to Know as Fallout Widens." *The New York Times*, The New York Times, 19 Mar. 2018, www.nytimes.com/2018/03/19/technology/facebook-cambridge-analytica-explained.html.

9. D'Onfro, Jillian, and Courtney Reagan. "Facebook's Marketing VP Says the Company Is 'beyond Disturbed' by Data Scandal." *USA Today*, Gannett Satellite Information Network, 20 Mar. 2018, www.usatoday.com/story/tech/2018/03/20/facebooks-marketing-vp-company-beyond-disturbed-data-scandal/440985002/.

10. Darcy, Oliver. "Facebook Removes Another 800 Pages and Accounts Ahead of Midterms." *CNN*, Cable News Network, 11 Oct. 2018, www.cnn.

com/2018/10/11/tech/facebook-removes-pages/index.html.

11. Botsman, Rachel. *Who Can You Trust?: How Technology Brought Us Together and Why It Might Drive Us Apart.* PublicAffairs, 2018.

12. Jong, Bart A. De, et al. "Trust and Team Performance: A Meta-Analysis of Main Effects, Moderators, and Covariates." *Journal of Applied Psychology*, vol. 101, no. 8, 2016, pp. 1134–1150., doi:10.1037/apl0000110.

13. "The Economics of Trust." *Chief Learning Officer - CLO Media*, 21 Aug. 2018, www.clomedia.com/2008/12/26/the-economics-of-trust/.

14. Spicer, Sean, and White House. "From the Archives: Sean Spicer on Inauguration Day Crowds." *@Politifact*, 21 Jan. 2017, www.politifact.com/truth-o-meter/statements/2017/jan/21/sean-spicer/trump-had-biggest-inaugural-crowd-ever-metrics-don/.

15. "Nearly 31 Million Americans Watch President Donald Trump's Inauguration." *What People Watch, Listen To and Buy*, www.nielsen.com/us/en/insights/news/2017/nearly-31-million-americans-watch-president-donald-trumps-inauguration.html.

16. Hains, Tim. "Chuck Todd to Kellyanne Conway: 'Alternative Facts Are Not Facts.'" *Video | RealClearPolitics*, RealClearPolitics, www.realclearpolitics.com/video/2017/01/22/chuck_todd_to_kellyanne_conway_alternative_facts_are_not_facts.html.

17. Geggis, Anne. "Stoneman Douglas Survivors Describe Scenes of Carnage in the Classrooms Targeted by Shooter." *Sun-Sentinel.com*, 12 Mar. 2018, www.sun-sentinel.com/local/broward/parkland/florida-school-shooting/fl-florida-school-shooting-class-posts-twitter-20180311-story.html.

18. Hayes, Christal. "Emma Gonzalez Survived the Florida Shooting. Now She's Taking on Trump and the NRA." *USA Today*, Gannett Satellite Information Network, 19 Feb. 2018, www.usatoday.com/story/news/2018/02/17/student-emma-gonzalez-school-shooting-gives-passionate-speech-against-g/348357002/.

19. Mazzei, Patricia. "Sheriff's Deputy Defends Actions in Florida Shooting, Denying He Was a 'Coward.'" *The New York Times*, The New York Times, 26 Feb. 2018, www.nytimes.com/2018/02/26/us/sheriffs-deputy-florida-shooting.html.

20. Madan, Monique O. "'It's All Crap.' Parents Lash out in Anger after Parkland Cop Scot Peterson Ends Silence." *Miamiherald*, Miami Herald, www.miamiherald.com/news/local/community/broward/article212483719.html.

21. FactCheck.org. "No 'Crisis Actors' in Parkland, Florida." *FactCheck.org*, 23 Feb. 2018, www.factcheck.org/2018/02/no-crisis-actors-parkland-florida/.

22. Breuninger, Kevin. "Advertisers Including Nestle Are Dumping Laura Ingraham after She Slammed Parkland Survivor David Hogg." *CNBC*, CNBC, 30 Mar. 2018, www.cnbc.com/2018/03/29/tripadvisor-drops-laura-ingraham-af-

ter-she-attacked-parkland-activist.html.

CHAPTER TWO

1. Stewart, Emily. "Watch: Dozens of Local TV Anchors Read the Same Anti-'False News' Script in Unison." *Vox.com*, Vox Media, 2 Apr. 2018, www.vox.com/ policy-and-politics/2018/4/2/17189302/sinclair-broadcast-fake-news-biased-trump-viral-video.

2. Turley, Jonathan. "Repealing the Second Amendment Isn't Easy but It's What March for Our Lives Students Need." *USA Today*, Gannett Satellite Information Network, 28 Mar. 2018, www.usatoday.com/story/opinion/2018/03/28/repealing-second-amendment-march-our-lives-students/463644002/.

3. Mezzofiore, Gianluca. "No, Emma Gonzalez Did Not Tear up a Photo of the Constitution." *CNN*, Cable News Network, 26 Mar. 2018, www.cnn. com/2018/03/26/us/emma-gonzalez-photo-doctored-trnd/index.html.

4. Diaz, Daniella. "6 Key Things Rubio Said on Guns at CNN Town Hall." *CNN*, Cable News Network, 22 Feb. 2018, www.cnn.com/2018/02/22/politics/marco-rubio-gun-debate-cnn-town-hall/index.html.

5. Sanchez, Luis. "DC Congresswoman Calls Rubio a Hypocrite over Age Limits for Rifle Purchases." *TheHill*, The Hill, 3 Apr. 2018, thehill.com/homenews/ senate/381430-dc-official-calls-rubio-a-hypocrite-for-claiming-he-supports-banning-minors.

6. Samuels, Brett. "Trump: 'So Many Signs That Florida Shooter Was Mentally Disturbed.'" *TheHill*, The Hill, 15 Feb. 2018, thehill.com/homenews/adminis-tration/373964-trump-so-many-signs-that-florida-shooter-was-mentally-dis-turbed.

7. Calia, Mike. "Trump Tweet: FBI Was Too Focused on Russia Probe to Notice Signs Leading to Florida School Massacre." *CNBC*, CNBC, 18 Feb. 2018, www. cnbc.com/2018/02/18/trump-fbi-missed-signals-for-florida-massacre-due-to-russia-probe.html.

8. "Here's What Dick's Sporting Goods CEO Ed Stack Wrote about His Company's Actions." *USA Today*, Gannett Satellite Information Network, 28 Feb. 2018, www.usatoday.com/story/money/retail/2018/02/28/heres-what-dicks-sporting-goods-ceo-ed-stack-wrote-his-companys-actions/381452002/.

9. McCurry, Justin. "Samsung Boss Faces Arrest as South Korea Corruption Scandal Grows." *The Guardian*, Guardian News and Media, 16 Jan. 2017, www. theguardian.com/world/2017/jan/16/samsung-boss-faces-arrest-as-south-ko-rea-corruption-scandal-grows.

10. "Samsung Heir Takes Stand to Deny Corruption Charges." *News24*, 2 Aug. 2017,

www.news24.com/World/News/samsung-heir-takes-stand-to-deny-corruption-charges-20170802.

11. "Samsung Scandal: Who Is Lee Jae-Yong?" *BBC News*, BBC, 5 Feb. 2018, www.bbc.com/news/business-39191196.

12. "Carthago Delenda Est." *Wikipedia*, Wikimedia Foundation, 21 Nov. 2018, en.wikipedia.org/wiki/Carthago_delenda_est.

13. "Comparing Hillary Clinton, Donald Trump on the Truth-O-Meter." *@Politifact*, www.politifact.com/truth-o-meter/lists/people/comparing-hillary-clinton-donald-trump-truth-o-met/.

14. Hasher, Lynn, et al. "Frequency and the Conference of Referential Validity." *Journal of Verbal Learning and Verbal Behavior*, vol. 16, no. 1, 1977, pp. 107–112., doi:10.1016/s0022-5371(77)80012-1.

15. Pennycook, Gordon, et al. "Prior Exposure Increases Perceived Accuracy of Fake News." *Journal of Experimental Psychology: General*, 2018, doi:10.1037/xge0000465.

16. Debruine, L. M. "Facial Resemblance Enhances Trust." *Proceedings of the Royal Society B: Biological Sciences*, vol. 269, no. 1498, July 2002, pp. 1307–1312., doi:10.1098/rspb.2002.2034.

17. Hunt, Vivian, et al. "Delivering through Diversity." *McKinsey & Company*, www.mckinsey.com/business-functions/organization/our-insights/delivering-through-diversity.

18. Cacioppo, John T., et al. "The Negativity Bias: Conceptualization, Quantification, and Individual Differences." *Behavioral and Brain Sciences*, vol. 37, no. 03, 2014, pp. 309–310., doi:10.1017/s0140525x13002537.

19. Kahneman, Daniel, and Amos Tversky. "Prospect Theory. An Analysis of Decision Making Under Risk." Jan. 1977, doi:10.21236/ada045771.

20. Streitfeld, David. "For Fact-Checking Website Snopes, a Bigger Role Brings More Attacks." *The New York Times*, The New York Times, 25 Dec. 2016, www.nytimes.com/2016/12/25/technology/for-fact-checking-website-snopes-a-bigger-role-brings-more-attacks.html.

21. Funke, Daniel. "Snopes Is Feuding with One of the Internet's Most Notorious Hoaxers." *Poynter*, 2 Aug. 2018, www.poynter.org/news/snopes-feuding-one-internets-most-notorious-hoaxers.

22. "Hard Questions: How Is Facebook's Fact-Checking Program Working?" *Facebook Newsroom*, Facebook Newsroom, newsroom.fb.com/news/2018/06/hard-questions-fact-checking/.

23. Fader, Carole. "Fact Check: So Who's Checking the Fact-Finders? We Are." *The Florida Times*, The Florida Times-Union, 28 Sept. 2012, www.jacksonville.com/article/20120928/NEWS/801246493.

24. "Striving for Ubuntu." *Desmond Tutu Foundation USA*, 21 Oct. 2015, www.tutufoundationusa.org/2015/10/06/striving-for-ubuntu/.

25. Mineo, Liz. "Over Nearly 80 Years, Harvard Study Has Been Showing How to Live a Healthy and Happy Life." *Harvard Gazette*, Harvard Gazette, 24 July 2018, news.harvard.edu/gazette/story/2017/04/over-nearly-80-years-harvard-study-has-been-showing-how-to-live-a-healthy-and-happy-life/.

26. "The Big Lesson Silicon Valley Can Learn From the Theranos Scandal." Fortune, Fortune, fortune.com/2018/03/15/elizabeth-holmes-theranos-fraud-secrecy/.

27. Lee, Bruce Y. "Theranos Could Have Avoided Recent Problems By Engaging The Scientific Community." *Forbes*, Forbes Magazine, 31 Mar. 2016, www.forbes.com/sites/brucelee/2016/03/31/theranos-could-have-avoided-recent-prob-lems-by-engaging-the-scientific-community/#4e87b9e16027.

28. Auletta, Ken. "Blood, Simpler." *The New Yorker*, The New Yorker, 19 June 2017, www.newyorker.com/magazine/2014/12/15/blood-simpler.

29. Sheetz, Michael. "Secretary DeVos, Walmart Heirs and Other Investors Reportedly Lost over $600 Million on Theranos." *CNBC*, CNBC, 4 May 2018, www.cnbc.com/2018/05/04/theranos-devos-other-investors-reported-ly-lost-over-600-million.html.

30. "Theranos' Board: Plenty of Political Connections, Little Relevant Expertise." Fortune, Fortune, fortune.com/2015/10/15/theranos-board-leadership/.

31. Johnson, Carolyn Y. "Trump's Pick for Defense Secretary Went to the Mat for the Troubled Blood-Testing Company Theranos." *The Washington Post*, WP Company, 1 Dec. 2016, www.washingtonpost.com/news/wonk/wp/2016/12/01/trumps-pick-for-defense-secretary-went-to-the-mat-for-the-troubled-blood-testing-company-theranos.

32. Ramsey, Lydia. "The FDA's Notes from Its Visit to Theranos' Labs Don't Look Good." *Business Insider*, Business Insider, 27 Oct. 2015, www.businessinsider.com/fda-documents-on-theranos-2015-10.

CHAPTER THREE

1. Carreyrou, John. "Hot Startup Theranos Has Struggled With Its Blood-Test Technology." *The Wall Street Journal*, Dow Jones & Company, 16 Oct. 2015, www.wsj.com/articles/theranos-has-struggled-with-blood-tests-1444881901.

2. Weaver, Christopher. "Theranos Agrees Not to Operate Blood Lab for Two Years." *The Wall Street Journal*, Dow Jones & Company, 18 Apr. 2017, www.wsj.com/articles/theranos-agrees-not-to-operate-blood-lab-for-two-years-1492472259.

3. "The Theranos Deception." *CBS News*, CBS Interactive, www.cbsnews.com/news/the-theranos-elizabeth-holmes-deception/.

4. "STUDY: Fake News Hits The Workplace." *Leadership IQ*, www.leadershipiq.com/blogs/leadershipiq/study-fake-news-hits-the-workplace.

5. "Dick Kazmaier." *Wikipedia*, Wikimedia Foundation, 8 Aug. 2018, en.wikipedia.org/wiki/Dick_Kazmaier.

6. Hastorf, Albert H., and Hadley Cantril. "They Saw a Game; a Case Study." *The Journal of Abnormal and Social Psychology*, vol. 49, no. 1, 1954, pp. 129–134., doi:10.1037/h0057880.

7. Asch, Solomon E. "Group Forces in the Modification and Distortion of Judgments." *Social Psychology.*, pp. 450–501., doi:10.1037/10025-016.

8. FOXBusiness. "Theranos' Chaotic Descent, as Told by Employees." *Fox Business*, Fox Business, 15 Mar. 2018, www.foxbusiness.com/features/theranos-chaotic-descent-as-told-by-employees.

9. Locklear, Mallory. "Theranos' Video Game Stars the Reporter Who Exposed the Company." *Engadget*, 1 May 2018, www.engadget.com/2018/04/19/theranos-video-game-stars-investigative-journalist/.

10. "VC Draper: Theranos Founder Elizabeth Holmes Was Bullied into Submission." *CNBC*, CNBC, 10 May 2018, www.cnbc.com/video/2018/05/10/vc-draper-theranos-founder-elizabeth-holmes-was-bullied-into-submission.html.

11. "Opinions and Social Pressure." *Nature*, vol. 176, no. 4491, 1955, pp. 1009–1011., doi:10.1038/1761009b0.

12. "Bay of Pigs Invasion: Kennedy's Cuban Catastrophe." *History Extra*, 19 Nov. 2018, www.historyextra.com/period/20th-century/bay-of-pigs-invasion-kennedys-cuban-catastrophe/.

13. Sidey, Hugh. "The Lesson John Kennedy Learned From the Bay of Pigs." *Time*, Time Inc., 16 Apr. 2001, content.time.com/time/nation/article/0,8599,106537,00.html.

14. Whitcomb, John, and Claire Whitcomb. *Real Life at the White House: Two Hundred Years of Daily Life at America's Most Famous Residence*. Routledge, 2002.

15. Janis, Irving Lester. *Victims of Groupthink: a Psychological Study of Foreignpolicy Decisions and Fiascoes*. Houghton Mifflin, 1974.

16. "This CEO Is out for Blood." *Fortune*, Fortune, fortune.com/2014/06/12/theranos-blood-holmes/.

17. "A Singular Board at Theranos." *Fortune*, Fortune, fortune.com/2014/06/12/theranos-board-directors/.

18. Sherif, Muzafer. *The Robbers Cave Experiment: Intergroup Conflict and Cooperation*. Wesleyan University Press, 1988.

19. Palmquist, Matt. "What Can the Cola Wars Teach Us about Brand Loyalty?" *Strategy Business*, 25 Aug. 2016, www.strategy-business.com/blog/What-Can-the-Cola-Wars-Teach-Us-about-Brand-Loyalty.

20. "The Cola Wars Get Personal." *CNNMoney*, Cable News Network, money.cnn.com/2003/06/13/news/funny/coke_pepsi/.

21. @aliceparkny, Alice Park. "Goodbye, Big Soda: New York Becomes First City to Ban Large-Sized Soft Drinks." *Time*, Time, 13 Sept. 2012, healthland.time.com/2012/09/13/goodbye-big-soda-new-york-becomes-first-city-to-ban-large-sized-soft-drinks/.

22. "Coke and Pepsi Have Joined Forces." *American Corporate Partners*, www.acp-usa.org/news/news/coke-and-pepsi-have-joined-forces-0.

23. Thompson, Krissah, and Scott Wilson. "Obama on Trayvon Martin: 'If I Had a Son, He'd Look like Trayvon.'" *The Washington Post*, WP Company, 23 Mar. 2012, www.washingtonpost.com/politics/obama-if-i-had-a-son-hed-look-like-trayvon/2012/03/23/gIQApKPpVS_story.html.

24. Graeff, Erhardt, et al. "The Battle for 'Trayvon Martin': Mapping a Media Controversy Online and off-Line." *First Monday*, vol. 19, no. 2, Mar. 2014, doi:10.5210/fm.v19i2.4947.

25. Wason, P. C. "On the Failure to Eliminate Hypotheses in a Conceptual Task." *Quarterly Journal of Experimental Psychology*, vol. 12, no. 3, 1960, pp. 129–140., doi:10.1080/17470216008416717.

26. Lord, Charles G., et al. "Biased Assimilation and Attitude Polarization: The Effects of Prior Theories on Subsequently Considered Evidence." *Journal of Personality and Social Psychology*, vol. 37, no. 11, 1979, pp. 2098–2109., doi:10.1037//0022-3514.37.11.2098.

27. Liu, Joseph. "Growing Number of Americans Say Obama Is a Muslim." *Pew Research Center's Religion & Public Life Project*, Pew Research Center's Religion & Public Life Project, 19 Mar. 2014, www.pewforum.org/2010/08/18/growing-number-of-americans-say-obama-is-a-muslim/.

28. Nyhan, Brendan, and Jason Reifler. "When Corrections Fail: The Persistence of Political Misperceptions." *Political Behavior*, vol. 32, no. 2, 2010, pp. 303–330., doi:10.1007/s11109-010-9112-2.

29. Broder, John M. "Stalled Out on Tesla's Electric Highway." *The New York Times*, The New York Times, 19 Oct. 2018, www.nytimes.com/2013/02/10/automobiles/stalled-on-the-ev-highway.html.

30. DeBord, Matthew. "Tesla Owners Criticizing Autopilot Have Unrealistic Expectations." *Business Insider*, Business Insider, 21 Apr. 2017, www.businessinsider.com/tesla-autopilot-class-action-suit-2017-4.

31. Weissman, Cale Guthrie. "Tesla Calls Journalism Nonprofit an 'Extremist

Organization' after Negative Story." *Fast Company*, Fast Company, 17 Apr. 2018, www.fastcompany.com/40560294/tesla-calls-journalism-nonprofit-an-extremist-organization-after-negative-story.

CHAPTER FOUR

1. Padilla, Raymond. "(Some) Tesla Fans Are the Worst." *RPad.TV*, 23 Sept. 2018, rpad.tv/2018/09/23/some-tesla-fans-are-the-worst/.

2. Adam Withnall @adamwithnall. "The Awful Story of How Aylan Kurdi Came to Be Washed up on a Turkish Beach." *The Independent*, Independent Digital News and Media, 22 Sept. 2015, www.independent.co.uk/news/world/europe/aylan-kurdi-s-story-how-a-small-syrian-child-came-to-be-washed-up-on-a-beach-in-turkey-10484588.html.

3. Shalby, Colleen. "A Crying Toddler Has Become the Symbolic Face of Family Separations. Does Her Backstory Matter?" Los Angeles Times, Los Angeles Times, 22 June 2018, www.latimes.com/nation/la-na-photo-migrant-girl-20180622-story.html.

4. McKay, Hollie. "Paul McCartney: Yoko Ono Didn't Break up the Beatles." *Fox News*, FOX News Network, www.foxnews.com/entertainment/paul-mccartney-yoko-ono-didnt-break-up-the-beatles.

5. "Scapegoat (n.)." *Index*, www.etymonline.com/word/scapegoat.

6. "A Psychological View of Conscience." *Collected Works of C.G. Jung, Volume 10: Civilization in Transition*, doi:10.1515/9781400850976.437.

7. Morgan, David. "Volkswagen's U.S. Chief Blames Emissions Scandal on 'Individuals.'" *Reuters*, Thomson Reuters, 8 Oct. 2015, www.reuters.com/article/volkswagen-emissions-congress-update-2-p-idUSL1N1281B720151008.

8. Cremer, Andreas, et al. "Reports: VW Warned about Illegal Emissions Tricks Many Years Ago." *Stltoday.com*, STLtoday.com, 27 Sept. 2015, www.stltoday.com/business/local/reports-vw-warned-about-illegal-emissions-tricks-many-years-ago/article_302e74e4-8e2d-56fe-a5ca-bfb484683d67.html.

9. "Two Views of the Same News Find Opposite Biases." *The Washington Post*, WP Company, 24 July 2006, www.washingtonpost.com/wp-dyn/content/article/2006/07/23/AR2006072300512.html.

10. Jenner, Kylie. "Sooo Does Anyone Else Not Open Snapchat Anymore? Or Is It Just Me... Ugh This Is so Sad." *Twitter*, Twitter, 21 Feb. 2018, twitter.com/kyliejenner/status/966429897118728192?lang=en.

11. "Consumer Sentiment toward Snapchat Drops Following Redesign." *YouGov*, today.yougov.com/topics/technology/articles-reports/2018/05/10/consum-

er-sentiment-drops-snapchat-redesign.

12. "Evan Spiegel." *Wikipedia*, Wikimedia Foundation, 19 Nov. 2018, en.wikipedia. org/wiki/Evan_Spiegel.

13. "Snapchat." *Wikipedia*, Wikimedia Foundation, 24 Nov. 2018, en.wikipedia.org/ wiki/Snapchat.

14. Kuchler, Hannah. "Evan Spiegel, Stanford Dropout with a Magic Touch." *Financial Times*, Financial Times, 14 July 2017, www.ft.com/content/1daaafc4-67b4-11e7-8526-7b38dcaef614.

15. Vengattil, Paresh Dave and Munsif. "UPDATE 1-Snap Beats on Revenue, Loses Users for the First Time." *CNBC*, CNBC, 7 Aug. 2018, www.cnbc. com/2018/08/07/reuters-america-update-1-snap-beats-on-revenue-loses-users-for-the-first-time.html.

16. *Bloomberg.com*, Bloomberg, www.bloomberg.com/news/features/2018-08-22/ nobody-trusts-facebook-twitter-is-a-hot-mess-what-is-snap-s-evan-spiegel-doing.

17. Wagner, Kurt. "Snap CEO Evan Spiegel: Facebook Can Copy Our Features, but 'Our Values Are Hard to Copy'." *Recode*, Recode, 30 May 2018, www.recode. net/2018/5/29/17384680/evan-spiegel-snap-ceo-code-conference-facebook-copy.

18. Meyer, Ashley N. D., et al. "Physicians' Diagnostic Accuracy, Confidence, and Resource Requests." *JAMA Internal Medicine*, vol. 173, no. 21, 2013, p. 1952., doi:10.1001/jamainternmed.2013.10081.

19. *Bloomberg.com*, Bloomberg, www.bloomberg.com/news/features/2018-08-22/ nobody-trusts-facebook-twitter-is-a-hot-mess-what-is-snap-s-evan-spiegel-doing.

20. Vosoughi, Soroush, et al. "The Spread of True and False News Online." *Science*, vol. 359, no. 6380, Aug. 2018, pp. 1146–1151., doi:10.1126/science.aap9559.

21. Kershner, Isabel. "Pardon Plea by Adolf Eichmann, Nazi War Criminal, Is Made Public." *The New York Times*, The New York Times, 19 Jan. 2018, www.nytimes. com/2016/01/28/world/middleeast/israel-adolf-eichmann-holocaust.html.

22. Milgram, Stanley. "The Perils of Obedience." Harper's Magazine, harpers.org/ archive/1973/12/the-perils-of-obedience/.

23. "Milgram Experiment." *Wikipedia*, Wikimedia Foundation, 16 Nov. 2018, en.wikipedia.org/wiki/Milgram_experiment.

24. Milgram, Stanley, and Philip G. Zimbardo. *Obedience to Authority: an Experimental View*. Printer & Martin, 2013.

25. "Resignations of 22 Umpires Stand, to Receive Termination Pay." *ESPN.com*, assets.espn.go.com/mlb/news/1999/0902/22170.html.

26. Martin, Douglas. "Richie Phillips, Union Leader Who Helped and Hurt Umpires, Dies at 72." *The New York Times*, The New York Times, 19 Oct. 2018, www.nytimes.com/2013/06/05/sports/baseball/richie-phillips-union-leader-who-helped-and-hurt-umpires-dies-at-72.html.

27. "Red Swoosh." *Wikipedia*, Wikimedia Foundation, 10 Sept. 2017, en.wikipedia.org/wiki/Red_Swoosh.

CHAPTER FIVE

1. "Uber." *Wikipedia*, Wikimedia Foundation, 25 Nov. 2018, en.wikipedia.org/wiki/Uber.

2. "Reflecting on One Very, Very Strange Year at Uber." *Susan Fowler*, 19 Feb. 2017, www.susanjfowler.com/blog/2017/2/19/reflecting-on-one-very-strange-year-at-uber.

3. Isaac, Mike. "Uber's C.E.O. Plays With Fire." *The New York Times*, The New York Times, 23 Apr. 2017, www.nytimes.com/2017/04/23/technology/travis-kalanick-pushes-uber-and-himself-to-the-precipice.html.

4. Lutz, Ashley. "Furious Customers Are Deleting the Uber App after Drivers Went to JFK Airport during a Protest and Strike." *Business Insider*, Business Insider, 29 Jan. 2017, www.businessinsider.com/delete-uber-hashtag-jfk-airport-taxi-strikes-2017-1.

5. Wong, Julia Carrie. "Uber Executive Fired amid Reports He Obtained Rape Victim's Medical Records." *The Guardian*, Guardian News and Media, 7 June 2017, www.theguardian.com/technology/2017/jun/07/uber-executive-fired-eric-alexander-rape-case-india.

6. "Stanford Prison Experiment." Encyclopedia of Group Processes & Intergroup Relations, doi:10.4135/9781412972017.n259.

7. "Stanford Prison Experiment: The 1971 Role Playing of Guards and Prisoners Brought out More Darkness than Expected." *The Vintage News*, The Vintage News, 11 July 2017, www.thevintagenews.com/2017/07/12/stanford-prison-experiment-the-1971-role-playing-of-guards-and-prisoners-brought-out-more-darkness-than-expected/.

8. Zimbardo, Philip. *The Lucifer Effect: Understanding How Good People Turn Evil.* Random House, 2013.

9. Farrow, Ronan. "From Aggressive Overtures to Sexual Assault: Harvey Weinstein's Accusers Tell Their Stories." *The New Yorker*, The New Yorker, 31 May 2018, www.newyorker.com/news/news-desk/from-aggressive-overtures-to-sexual-assault-harvey-weinsteins-accusers-tell-their-stories.

10. Kantor, Jodi, and Megan Twohey. "Harvey Weinstein Paid Off Sexual Harassment Accusers for Decades." *The New York Times*, The New York Times, 5 Oct. 2017, www.nytimes.com/2017/10/05/us/harvey-weinstein-harassment-allegations.html.

11. Flitter, Emily. "The Former Khmer Rouge Slave Who Blew the Whistle on Wells Fargo." *The New York Times*, The New York Times, 24 Mar. 2018, www.nytimes.com/2018/03/24/business/wells-fargo-whistleblower-duke-tran.html.

12. Randall. "Wells Fargo Whistle Blower Wins Huge Settlement." AsAm News, 28 Mar. 2018, asamnews.com/2018/03/26/wells-fargo-whistle-blower-wins-huge-settlement/.

13. Hardy, Kevin. "'Rebuilding Trust Is Our Top Priority,' Wells Fargo CEO Pledges." *Des Moines Register*, The Des Moines Register, 25 Apr. 2018, www.desmoinesregister.com/story/money/business/2018/04/24/wells-fargo-des-moines-scandal-shareholder-meeting-trust-ceo-tim-sloan/545678002/.

14. "A Quote by William Gibson." *Goodreads*, Goodreads, www.goodreads.com/quotes/681-the-future-is-already-here-it-s-just-not-evenly.

15. Mistreanu, Simina. "China Is Implementing a Massive Plan to Rank Its Citizens, and Many of Them Want in." *Foreign Policy*, Foreign Policy, 3 Apr. 2018, foreignpolicy.com/2018/04/03/life-inside-chinas-social-credit-laboratory/.

16. Ming, Cheang. "Shorter Airport Lines for Some, Travel Bans for Others: China's Systematic Social Scorekeeping." *CNBC*, CNBC, 17 Mar. 2017, www.cnbc.com/2017/03/16/china-social-credit-system-ant-financials-sesame-credit-and-others-give-scores-that-go-beyond-fico.html.

17. Botsman, Rachel. "Big Data Meets Big Brother as China Moves to Rate Its Citizens." *WIRED*, WIRED UK, 4 June 2018, www.wired.co.uk/article/chinese-government-social-credit-score-privacy-invasion.

18. "Americans' Fear of Driverless Cars Subsiding: AAA Survey." *Insurance Journal*, 29 Jan. 2018, www.insurancejournal.com/news/national/2018/01/29/478685.htm.

19. Hsu, Tiffany. "Tesla Boosts Car Battery Power During Irma, Raising Questions of Control." *The New York Times*, The New York Times, 12 Sept. 2017, www.nytimes.com/2017/09/11/business/tesla-battery-irma-upgrade.html.

20. Wakefield, Jane. "The Man Who Was Fired by a Machine." *BBC News*, BBC, 21 June 2018, www.bbc.com/news/technology-44561838.

21. Dewan, Angela, and Joshua Berlinger. "Drop Charges against News Site Rappler, Human Rights Watch Says." *CNN*, Cable News Network, 30 Nov. 2018, www.cnn.com/2018/11/30/asia/maria-ressa-philippines-journalist-hrw-intl/index.html.

22. Felipe, Cecille Suerte. "PNP Bares Numbers: 4,251 Dead in Drug War."

Philstar.com, The Philippine Star, 7 May 2018, www.philstar.com/head-lines/2018/05/08/1813217/pnp-bares-numbers-4251-dead-drug-war.

23. "Critics Hit Duterte's Promise to Continue Campaign against Drugs." *UNTV News,* www.untvweb.com/videos/critics-hit-dutertes-promise-to-continue-campaign-against-drugs/.

24. Bremmer, Ian. "The Era of the Tough Guy Leader Is Here to Stay." Time, *Time,* 3 May 2018, time.com/5264170/the-strongmen-era-is-here-heres-what-it-means-for-you/.

25. Etter, Lauren. " What Happens When the Government Uses Facebook as a Weapon?" *Bloomberg.com,* 7 December 2017, www.bloomberg.com/news/features/2017-12-07/how-rodrigo-duterte-turned-facebook-into-a-weapon-with-a-little-help-from-facebook.

26. Arsenault, Adrienne. "'Democracy as We Know It Is Dead': Filipino Journalists Fight Fake News | CBC News." *CBCnews,* CBC/Radio Canada, 27 Apr. 2017, www.cbc.ca/news/world/democracy-as-we-know-it-is-dead-filipino-journalists-fight-fake-news-1.4086920.

27. Johnson, Eric. "Memo from a 'Facebook Nation' to Mark Zuckerberg: You Moved Fast and Broke Our Country." *Recode,* Recode, 26 Nov. 2018, www.recode.net/2018/11/26/18111859/maria-ressa-rappler-facebook-mark-zuckerberg-philippines-kara-swisher-recode-decode-podcast.

CHAPTER SIX

1. Dutta, Prabhash K. "Demonetisation: What India Gained, and Lost." *India Today,* India Today, 30 Aug. 2018, www.indiatoday.in/india/story/demonetisation-what-india-gained-and-lost-1327502-2018-08-30.

2. Singh, Sandeep. "After Demonetisation: As Cash Comes in, Digital Deals Show Sharp Dip." The Indian Express, The Indian Express, 4 Mar. 2017, indianexpress.com/article/india/demonetisation-digital-payments-online-transactions-cashless-economy-india-decline-in-electronic-transactions-4553410/.

3. Choudhury, Saheli Roy. "Google DeepMind, Humanity and a Freakishly Hard Game." *CNBC,* CNBC, 9 Mar. 2016, www.cnbc.com/2016/03/08/google-deep-minds-alphago-takes-on-go-champion-lee-sedol-in-ai-milestone-in-seoul.html.

4. Good, I. J. "The Mystery of Go." *Computer Games II,* 1988, pp. 87–93., doi:10.1007/978-1-4613-8754-1_9.

5. Zastrow, Mark. "How Victory for Google's Go AI Is Stoking Fear in South Korea." *New Scientist,* New Scientist, www.newscientist.com/article/2080927-how-victory-for-googles-go-ai-is-stoking-fear-in-south-korea/.

6. *Machines That Think: Everything You Need to Know about the Coming Age of Artificial Intelligence.* John Murray Learning, 2017.

7. Tech, Breitbart. "Rise of the Machines: Keep an Eye on AI, Say Experts." *Breitbart*, Breitbart News Network, 12 Mar. 2016, www.breitbart.com/tech/2016/03/12/rise-of-the-machines-keep-an-eye-on-ai-say-experts/.

8. Daugherty, Paul R., and H. James Wilson. *Human Machine: Reimagining Work in the Age of AI.* Harvard Business Review Press, 2018.

9. Haber, Stuart, and W. Scott Stornetta. "How to Time-Stamp a Digital Document." *Advances in Cryptology-CRYPT0' 90 Lecture Notes in Computer Science,* pp. 437–455., doi:10.1007/3-540-38424-3_32.

10. Bayer, Dave, et al. "Improving the Efficiency and Reliability of Digital Time-Stamping." *Sequences II,* 1993, pp. 329–334., doi:10.1007/978-1-4613-9323-8_24.

11. Lakhani, Marco IansitiKarim R., and Harvard Business Review. "The Truth About Blockchain." *Harvard Business Review,* 6 Mar. 2018, hbr.org/2017/01/the-truth-about-blockchain.

12. "The Promise of the Blockchain Technology." *The Economist,* The Economist Newspaper, 1 Sept. 2018, www.economist.com/technology-quarterly/2018/09/01/the-promise-of-the-blockchain-technology.

CONCLUSION

1. Brito, Christopher. "White House Accused of Sharing 'Doctored' Video of CNN Reporter, Intern Exchange." *CBS News,* CBS Interactive, 8 Nov. 2018, www.cbsnews.com/news/jim-acosta-sarah-sanders-cnn-reporter-white-house-intern-video-doctored/.

2. Potkin, Fanny. "Exclusive: Juul Sounds out Indonesia for Expansion, Other Asian..." Reuters, Thomson Reuters, 13 Nov. 2018, www.reuters.com/article/us-juul-expansion-asia-exclusive/exclusive-juul-sounds-out-indonesia-for-expansion-other-asian-countries-in-its-sights-idUSKCN1NI0HD.

3. *Bloomberg.com,* Bloomberg, www.bloomberg.com/news/features/2018-11-01/whatsapp-groups-and-misinformation-are-a-threat-to-fragile-democracies.

GLOSSARY OF TERMS USED

1. **Authority Bias:** The tendency to obey the orders of an authority figure, even when you don't agree with those orders.

2. **Backfire Effect:** A cognitive bias that causes people to reject evidence that challenges their beliefs, and to strengthen their support of their original stance.

3. **Confirmation Bias:** The tendency to search for, recall, and privilege information in a way that confirms our pre-existing beliefs or hypotheses.

4. **Conformity Bias:** The tendency to take cues for proper behavior from the actions of others rather than exercising our own independent, critical judgment.

5. **Familiarity Bias:** The pattern of expressing a preference for things simply because of familiarity with them.

6. **Groupthink:** The psychological phenomenon that occurs when

the desire for group harmony results in irrational or dysfunctional decision-making.

7. **Illusory Truth Effect**: The tendency to believe information to be correct after repeated exposure.

8. **Ingroup Bias:** A pattern of favoring members of one's in-group over members of an out-group.

9. **Inoculation Theory:** A technique used to make people immune to attempts to change their attitudes by exposing them to small arguments against their position.

10. **Naive Realism:** The tendency to believe that we see the world around us objectively and that people who disagree with us are uninformed, irrational, or biased.

11. **Negativity Bias:** The asymmetrical way in which negative experiences exert greater psychological impact on us than positive experiences of the same magnitude.

12. **Overconfidence Bias:** The tendency for our subjective confidence to be greater than the objective accuracy of those judgments.

13. **Post-Trust:** A breakdown in trust due to our inability to discern facts from opinions and outright fabrications.

14. **Post-Truth:** A state in which objective facts are less influential in shaping public opinion than appeals to emotion and personal belief.

15. **Trust Leaps:** The risk we take in doing something new or differently from the way it's been done in the past.

16. **Scapegoating:** The tendency to blame someone else for one's own failure or misdeeds, thereby maintaining one's positive self-image.

17. **Selective Perception:** The process by which we privilege information that supports our views while ignoring opposing viewpoints.

18. **Technocognition:** The idea that humans should use what we know of psychology to design technology in a way that minimizes the impact of misinformation.

INDEX